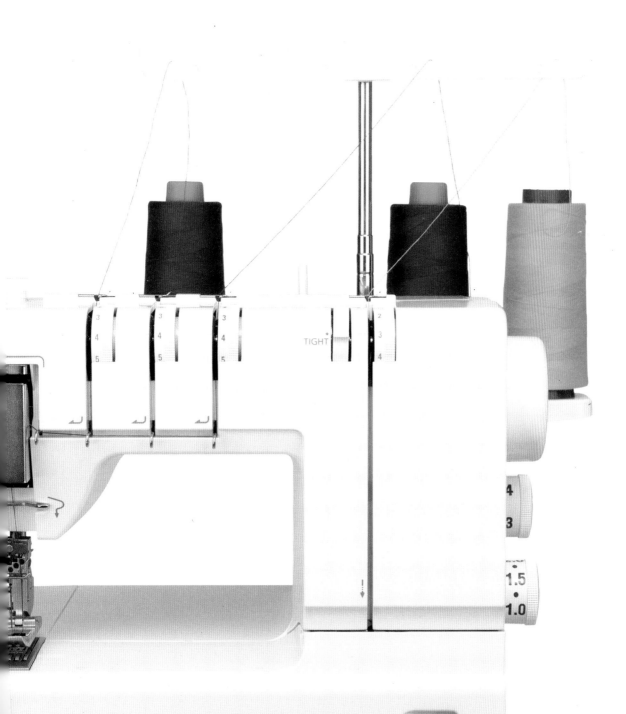

MASTER THE COVERSTITCH MACHINE

THE COMPLETE COVERSTITCH SEWING GUIDE

JOHANNA LUNDSTRÖM

To anyone who wants to master
the coverstitch and discover all the
amazing things you can do with
this machine

CONTENTS

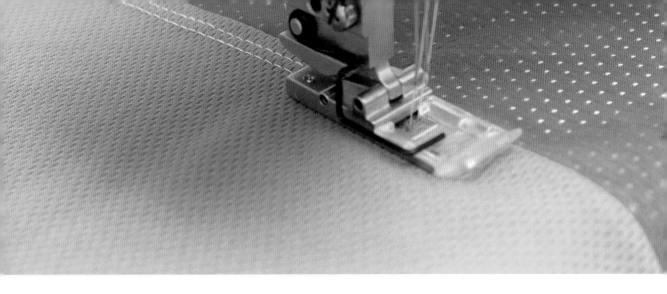

INTRODUCTION

I bought my first coverstitch machine in the early 2000s as I was eager to achieve a more professional finish on my knit garments. But I soon discovered that this machine is not as straightforward as I had initially thought. In fact, it took a lot of experimenting and learning from various experts in order to fully master this machine.

Drawing from my own experiences, I made this book for my fellow sewists who want to get more out of their coverstitch machine and discover all the fantastic things you can do with it. As this book will teach you, there is so much more we can do than just hemming knits.

And if you are one of those who has felt a certain coverstitch frustration from time to time, I'm here to help you! This book will teach you all the techniques required to enjoy a smooth coverstitch experience.

Happy sewing!

Johanna

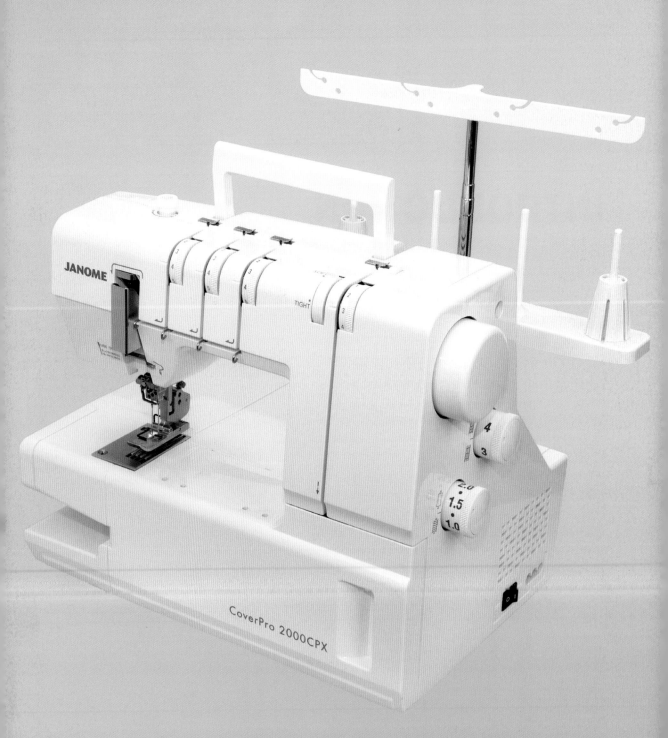

CHAPTER 1
MACHINE

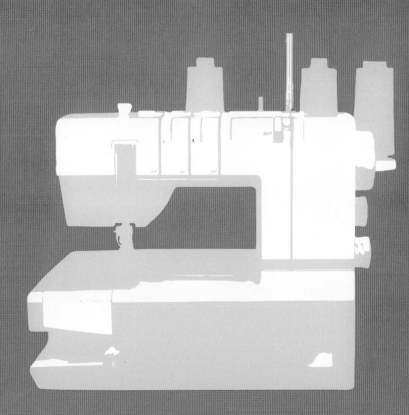

COVERSTITCH MODELS

For the domestic market, there are currently four different types of coverstitch machines available: 2-needle, 3-needle, a serger/coverstitch combination machine, and a top-cover machine.

MACHINE QUICK GUIDE

- **BASIC:** 2-needle coverstitch machine
- **STANDARD:** 3-needle coverstitch machine
- **SPACE SAVER:** Coverstitch/ serger combination machine
- **PRO:** Top-cover machine

2-needle coverstitch machine

Has 2 needles and 1 looper and can sew a 3-thread coverstitch and a single-row chainstitch seam. With this machine, you can hem knit garments with the classic 2-needle wide coverstitch seam that's also used to attach neckline binding and making belt loops on pants. Uses up to 3 thread cones.

3-needle coverstitch machine

Comes with slots for 3 needles and 1 looper. This is a very versatile machine, which can sew both a 2-needle wide and narrow coverstitch, a single needle chainstitch, and a 3-needle coverstitch seam. The 3-needle coverstitch seam also creates a very distinct reverse seam that is a popular choice to use as a decorative stitch on the right side of the fabric. The machine uses up to 4 thread cones.

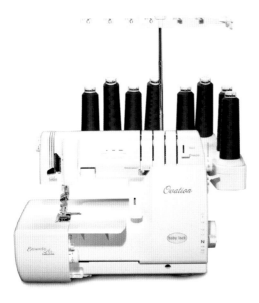

Coverstitch/serger combination machine

A combo machine can sew overlock, coverstitch, and chainstitch seams. They save space and possibly also money, although some combination machines are quite costly. On many combination machines, you might have to switch and rethread the set-up when you want to change between serging and coverstitching, which can take a few minutes.

The combo machine has either a 2- or 3-needle configuration and can sew all the seams a normal coverstitch machine and serger can sew. Many combination machines can also sew a safety stitch: that is, they sew a straight chainstitch and overlock the edges at the same time. Combination machines can hold 5 to 8 thread cones.

DID YOU KNOW?

- Most machines can sew a wide 2-needle coverstitch

- Only 3-needle machines can sew a narrow coverstitch

- Every coverstitch machine can sew a single needle chainstitch

- Some combo machines need to be converted in order to sew a coverstitch seam

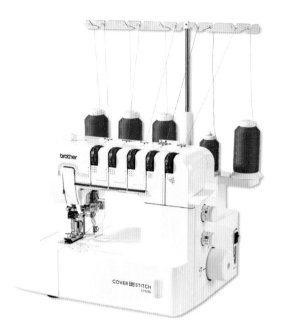

Top-cover machine

This coverstitch machine that can also sew a decorative double-sided coverstitch seam on both the front and reverse sides of the garment. The double-sided option is usually available both for 3-needle wide and 2-needle narrow and wide. This top-cover seam looks very similar to the industrial stitches used for knits and can be used for hemming, decorative topstitching, flat joining seams, and much more.

The double-sided coverstitch machine also sews a regular 2-needle wide and narrow coverstitch, a single needle chainstitch and a 3-needle coverstitch seam. It uses up to 5 thread cones.

COVERSTITCH BUYER'S GUIDE

A coverstitch machine will be a very useful addition to your sewing machine collection. If you are reading this book, you might already own one, but perhaps you are considering an upgrade?

Regardless of your situation, there are several factors to consider when buying a coverstitch machine.

Buy the best machine you can afford

As high-quality sewing machines are expensive, it can be tempting to look for budget options, such as a lower-quality serger/coverstitch combination machine.

But those can be cumbersome to use and the stitch quality is usually lower, not a good situation because reliable stitching is crucial when it comes to coverstitching. If your budget is tight, it is better to buy a high-quality, second-hand coverstitch machine.

The good news is that good quality coverstitch machines have great longevity and seldom break down, so an older, serviced, machine will still work like clockwork.

Try before you buy

These days, many people buy their sewing machines online, but if you have access to local sewing machine stores, take that opportunity to try several coverstitch machines before you settle on a model.

Buying a machine from a knowledgeable local seller can save you a lot of frustration and hassle later on, and some brands don't even allow their machines to be sold online.

What features do you need?

As outlined previously, there are four categories of machine: the regular machine, in either 2- or 3-needle versions; the top-cover machine; and the serger/coverstitch combination machine.

Make sure you put a lot of thought into considering what features you really need before buying.

Compare accessories

Most coverstitch machine brands sell a selection of accessories, including various presser feet, binder attachments, hem folding devices and seam guides. But those differ a lot from brand to brand; for instance, not all brands have a binder attachment or an elastic presser foot.

Some attachments are generic and can be used on different coverstitch brands and models, but others, such as presser feet, are machine specific and can't be substituted. So make sure you buy a model that has the accessories you want to use.

That said, a lot can be accomplished with just a regular presser foot, so unless you get a great package deal, don't go out and buy a ton of accessories before you have learned to use your machine properly and have assessed what you really need.

Does the seller offer classes?

Some sewing machine vendors offer classes when you purchase a machine. As in-person teaching is a very effective way to learn how to use a coverstitch machine, buying your machine from a vendor that offers classes is a very good idea.

Read reviews and check online sewing groups

These days, there is a myriad of coverstitch machine reviews available online, and there are also Facebook groups and other online communities where you can talk to other coverstitch users about their experience with various machines.

COVERSTITCH BRANDS

- BabyLock
- Juki
- Janome
- Singer
- Pfaff
- Elna
- Brother
- Necchi
- Bernina
- Bernette
- Husqvarna
- Joy

PARTS OF A COVERSTITCH

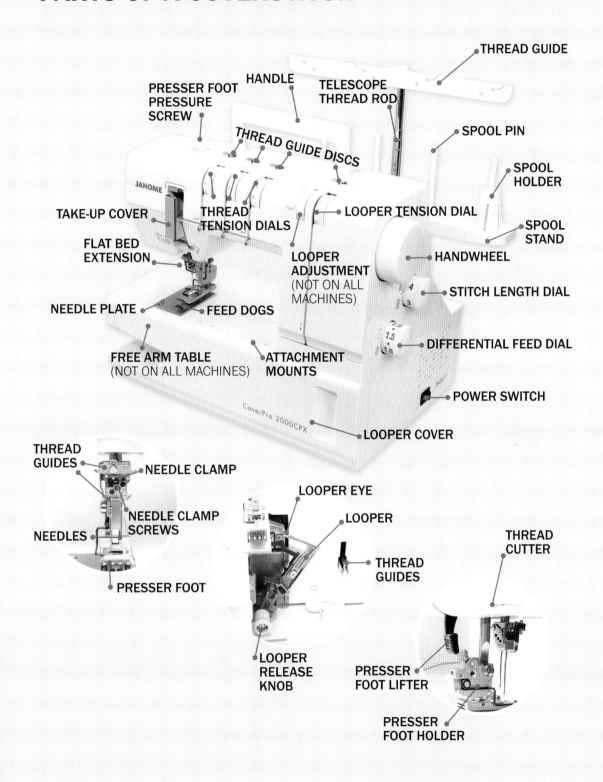

THREAD GUIDE

PRESSER FOOT PRESSURE SCREW

HANDLE

TELESCOPE THREAD ROD

SPOOL PIN

THREAD GUIDE DISCS

SPOOL HOLDER

TAKE-UP COVER

THREAD TENSION DIALS

LOOPER TENSION DIAL

SPOOL STAND

FLAT BED EXTENSION

LOOPER ADJUSTMENT (NOT ON ALL MACHINES)

HANDWHEEL

NEEDLE PLATE

FEED DOGS

STITCH LENGTH DIAL

FREE ARM TABLE (NOT ON ALL MACHINES)

ATTACHMENT MOUNTS

DIFFERENTIAL FEED DIAL

POWER SWITCH

CoverPro 2000CPX

LOOPER COVER

THREAD GUIDES

NEEDLE CLAMP

LOOPER EYE

LOOPER

THREAD CUTTER

NEEDLE CLAMP SCREWS

NEEDLES

THREAD GUIDES

PRESSER FOOT

LOOPER RELEASE KNOB

PRESSER FOOT LIFTER

PRESSER FOOT HOLDER

JANOME

COVERSTITCH MAINTENANCE

If you do have a problem, check the machine manual for what type of maintenance is recommended for home users. If that doesn't help, it's best to ... take your machine to a mechanic.

Unless you know what you are doing, dismantling the machine is not recommended — and it can also make the warranty void.

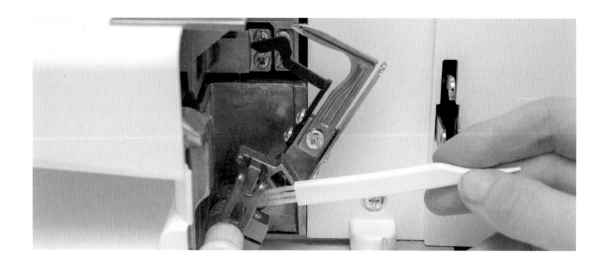

CLEANING THE COVERSTITCH

Keeping the machine clean is important for good stitch quality and it's something you can easily do at home.

TOOLS FOR CLEANING

Lint brush
These are usually included with the machine, but you can also use a good quality, soft hair, artist brush.

Mini-vacuum
It's not necessary, but good to have. These tools effectively remove lint in hard-to-reach places. Just make sure you buy a good one, as some models have very weak vacuum power.

Tweezers
A great tool for removing lint and threads that have become stuck in the tension discs and in the looper area. Use a pair of narrowly pointed tweezers.

CLEANING THE LOOPER AREA

The looper area is usually where you'll find the most lint, especially if you have a serger/coverstitch combination machine.

1. Unplug the machine

2. Open the looper cover

3. Remove all lint using your preferred tool

4. Usually, you will have to go over the parts with a brush too, in order to remove all the lint

5. Close the loop cover

6. Wipe your machine with a cloth to remove any dust and lint that has spread to the surface areas

CLEANING THE FEED DOGS AREA

Lint underneath the needle plate can cause wonky stitching, so make it a habit to keep that area clean.

1. Unplug the machine before cleaning

2. Remove the needles and presser foot

3. Remove the needle plate by releasing the screws (check the manual)

4. Clean the feed dogs using a brush

5. Attach the plate again

CLEANING THE TENSION DISCS

Lint and threads that get stuck in the tension discs can mess up the tension and create uneven stitching.

1. Release the tension by raising the presser foot

2. Set the discs to the lowest tension number

3. Use a brush to remove lint

4. Use tweezers to remove thread strands

5. Floss the tension dials. Regular dental floss can be used for this purpose

OILING THE COVERSTITCH

Most modern coverstitch machines are self-lubricating and the manufacturers usually advise against oiling the machine. This is why most coverstitch manuals do not include information about oiling parts of the machine. If you do decide to oil any part of the machine, be aware that you do so at your own risk.

If you still want to go against the advice of the manufacturers and do it yourself, go lightly on the oil, and stick to the few moving parts in the looper and feed dog area. It's also important to use only a high-quality sewing machine oil that is specifically recommended for coverstitch machines and sergers.

But remember that having a professional mechanic servicing your machine is a great investment when it comes to the longevity of your coverstitch.

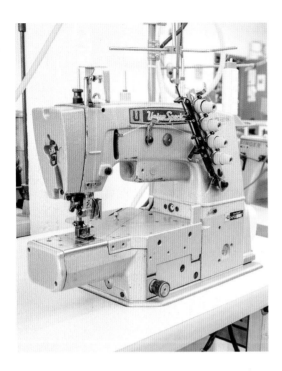 

Industrial coverstitching

Coverstitch machines are an important part of many modern garment factories. They are used for everything from sewing belt loops and topstitching jeans to attaching neckline binding and hemming knits.

But if you think industrial machines are more reliable compared with domestic ones, then think again.

"We struggle even though we often have a mechanic to help us", says machine operator Oili Saikkonen.

In the garment factory of Borås Textile University, there are seven coverstitch machines with different set-ups. Industrial coverstitch machines seldom have to multi-task. Instead, they usually are set for just doing one single thing, such as sewing belt loops or hemming knits.

Setting up a coverstitch machine and making sure it works well is tricky, so it saves a lot of time to have dedicated machines instead of needing to make changes to the set-up all the time.

"Most problems are either caused by faulty threading or the needle"

According to seasoned machine operators Oili Saikkonen and Jasna Caktas, the coverstitch machine is the most cumbersome machine to use of all sewing machines, as it is very sensitive to faulty threading and needle issues. So, for those who might think that an industrial machine would be better and more reliable than a home version, well, Oili cautions with a story to share:

"I was considering getting an industrial coverstitch machine to use at home, but our machine mechanic advised me not to, since they are so complicated and there are a many things that can go wrong".

COVERSTITCH LIKE A PRO

- **Always start by threading the looper.** Then thread one thread at a time, making sure the threads don't get tangled up with each other. Every needle thread needs to run separately.

- **Most problems are caused by the needle or faulty threading.** Check that the needle isn't broken and that it is placed properly in the bar slot. Then make sure the threading is done 100% correctly. The coverstitch machine is very sensitive and even the smallest threading errors can cause problems.

- **Use the right needle and size.** Always use ballpoint needles when coverstitching knit fabrics. In the industrial setting they use a size 70 for thin fabrics and 80 for medium knits.

- **Pick the right thread.** Use regular serger thread (120 dtex) for the needle threads and flossy stretch thread (160 dtex woolly nylon) in the looper. That will provide the best looking stitches when hemming knits.

- **Get the tension right.** Make sure the needle thread sits properly between the tension discs.

- **Troubleshoot.** Use different colour threads to troubleshoot where the problem lies.

- **Don't mess with a good thing.** Once you get the settings right, document them and don't tamper with the machine unless you have to!

WHY ARE INDUSTRIAL COVERSTITCH MACHINES HARDER TO USE?

Firstly threading an industrial coverstitch machine is often more complicated and less intuitive compared with a domestic machine. Plus the tension knobs often lack numbers, which makes it hard to document the settings. Instead, the machine operator often marks lines on the knobs and on the machine once they have found the perfect combination of settings, which is another reason why they sew the same thing over and over in the garment industry.

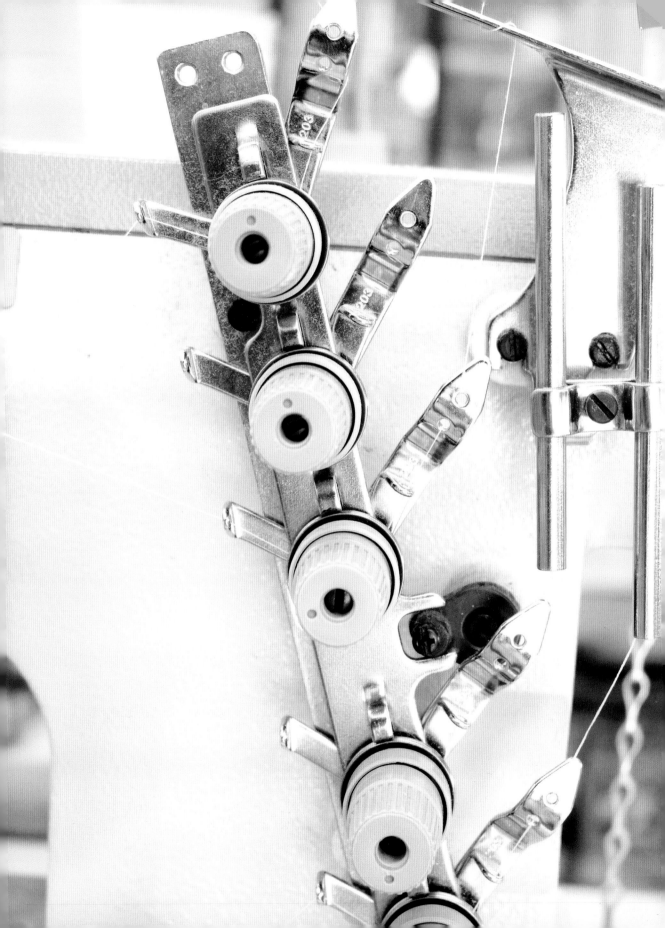

CHAPTER 2
TOOLS

MACHINE ACCESSORIES

Coverstitch machines usually come with an assortment of accessories. Here are the most common ones, which can also be bought separately if your machine lacks them.

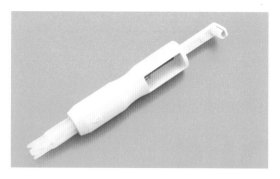

NEEDLE INSERTER AND THREADER
This multi-tool is used both to push the thread through the needle eye and to insert the needles into the needle bar.

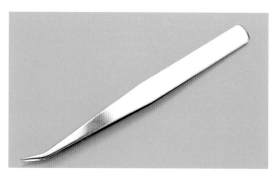

TWEEZERS
Angled tweezers are used for threading the looper and needles. They can also be used for inserting needles and removing lint and threads that are stuck in hard-to-reach areas.

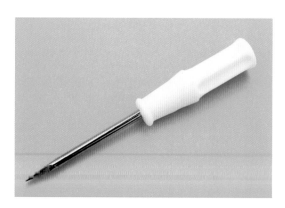

SCREWDRIVER
These are used the needle clamp screws. These small screwdrivers usually have a regular slot or a six-sided (hex) shape.

LINT BRUSH
This brush is used to remove lint and dust. It's the safest way to clean a coverstitch machine

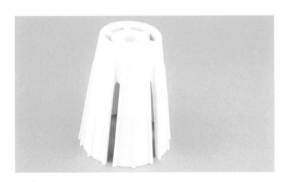

CONE HOLDER

This provides stability for the large thread cones used on a coverstitch machine. The holder is placed over the spool rod pin to keep the cone in place when sewing.

SPOOL NETS

These nets prevent the thread from getting stuck underneath the spool, slipping away or getting tangled.

SPOOL CAPS

These will make the thread reel freely and prevent it from getting caught in the rough spool edges when using traditional sewing machine thread spools on your serger.

SPECIALTY PRESSER FEET

Most coverstitch machines only come with a standard presser foot when purchased, but many brands also offer various Specialty feet that can be bought separately. These will, however, vary greatly from brand to brand, so not all feet listed here will be available for every type of machine.

Clear presser foot

A transparent foot that makes it easy to see the stitching. Useful for decorative stitching, attaching binding and when sewing over seams. The clear presser foot can replace the standard foot.

Edge guide presser foot

This foot has a blade in the middle that is used to align the presser foot against a seam line or a fabric edge. It makes stitching down seam allowances and stitching in the ditch easier.

Chainstitch presser foot

Foot designed specifically for sewing single row chainstitches. The presser foot is designed to move smoothly over the chainstitch and shaped so that the seam is easy to see while sewing.

Pintuck foot

For sewing pintucks on the coverstitch machine. It forms ridges between the needles, just like a pintuck presser foot for a regular sewing machine.

COVERSTITCH ATTACHMENTS

Binder attachment

Use for attaching bias tape and knit binding. This attachment comes in many variations and sizes and you can also find generic brands that can be used on your machine. As a rule of thumb, a narrow binding is more commonly used for children's clothing and a wider binding is more popular on garments made for adults.

Belt loop attachment

Folds narrow tape binder strips, such as belt loops, straps and drawstrings. It will either fold the strips so that the edges overlap or let the edges meet in the middle; the latter is common on industrially made belt loops. If your coverstitch machine brand doesn't have this tool, you can use a generic belt loop maker and attach it to the machine using Blu-Tack or tape.

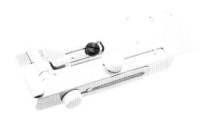

Elastic attachment

Comes with an adjustable guide where you place the elastic. This function keeps the elastic in place and also ensures that the stretch is evenly distributed. Tightening the screw on the guide will create more gathers and loosening will release the tension.

Fold and hem guides

These hem guides both fold and guide the fabric for even stitching. On some models you can adjust the width of the fold, but the height is usually fixed. So if the fabric is very thick, this attachment might not work.

ANATOMY OF A NEEDLE

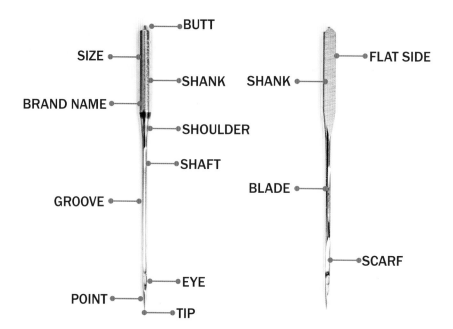

Butt: The slanted end of the needle.

Shank: The part that goes into the needle bar. The front shank is round and the back is flat on domestic sewing machine needles. On industrial needles, the shank is generally round all over with no flat sections.

Shoulder: The area between the shank and the blade.

Grooves: The grooves on the blade guide the thread to the eye. Some needles have additional grooves on the back of the blade, which help reduce skipped stitches and form the chainstitches.

Blade: The blade makes it easier for the needle to pierce through the fabric. The needle size is determined by the blade diameter.

Scarf: The dent above the eye allows the bobbin hook to easily catch the needle thread to create a stitch.

Eye: The hole through which the needle thread passes. Larger needles will have a bigger eye.

Point and tip: The area that enters the fabric first. The length, shape and size vary depending on the needle type. Universal needles have a slight ballpoint tip and stretch needles have a medium ballpoint tip.

NEEDLE SYSTEMS

Some coverstitch machines will be configured to use regular domestic sewing machine needles whereas others require specific serger needles or industrial needles, which is why it is important to use the recommended needle system for your machine. Don't experiment with the wrong needles!

Also, the length of the needles will vary depending on the system, and using the incorrect length can potentially damage the machine.

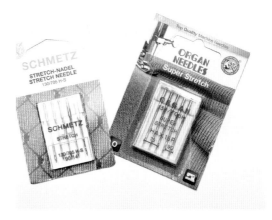

Serger needles

There are several needle systems for sergers, including Elx705 and DCX1 and DBX1. Serger needles are generally more durable and usually have grooves on both the front and back of the needle. This helps reduce skipped stitches and facilitates the formation of chainstitches, such as coverstitch stitches.

Most modern coverstitch machines are configured for serger needles, but there are exceptions, which is why consulting the manual is crucial.

Sewing machine needles

Common domestic sewing machine systems are 130/705H, 15x1, and HAX1. Normally, these can be used interchangeably and the codes are just brand variations for the same needle type. A domestic sewing machine needle has a smooth blade and is often slightly less reinforced than a serger needle.

Industrial needles

If you own or are considering buying an industrial machine, you need to use an industrial needle system. Most domestic needle brands also make needles for industrial machines. Common coverstitch needle systems are TVx3SES and UYX128GAS.

NEEDLE TYPES

In general, two types of needles are recommended for coverstitch machines; universal and ballpoint.

Universal

General purpose needles for both woven and knit fabrics. Unlike a needle that is made strictly for woven fabrics, a universal needle usually has a slight ballpoint tip, which is why it can also work for stitching knit fabrics.

Ballpoint

Has a rounded point that pushes the fibres aside instead of piercing holes in the fabric, which makes them great for knit fabrics. The needle has a medium ballpoint tip and works for most knit fabrics, and can also help prevent skipped stitches and snags. They are usually labelled as ballpoint, overlock or jersey needles.

Stretch ballpoint

If you are sewing a lot of stretch Spandex knits, a stretch ballpoint needle is a good option. They have a specially designed eye and scarf to prevent skipped stitches. These needles are often labelled 'Stretch' or 'Super stretch', but make sure that they correspond with the needle system on your coverstitch machine.

NEEDLE SIZES

The needle size is determined by the diameter of the needle blade, and it's important to pick a size that is optimal for both the machine and the project you are sewing.

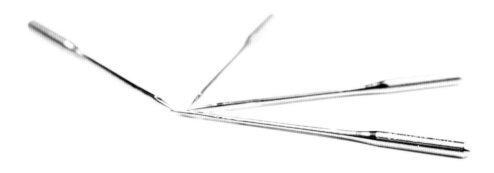

There are two common size systems for sewing machine needles: American and European. The smallest needles in the American system begin with a single digit (i.e., 8) and the European system starts with double digits (i.e., 60).

The actual size is, however, the same in both systems and is based on the diameter of the needle at a point just above the scarf. Many manufacturers show both systems in the description that is embossed in the shank (e.g., 60/8). The larger the needle is, the higher the number will be.

- For coverstitching, most machines are optimised for 80/12 and 90/14 size needles.

- Pick a smaller needle if you are sewing through very lightweight knit to avoid unsightly holes.

- Go for a larger needle if you are stitching over thicker layers, elastic, firm wovens, or if skipped stitches is a problem.

INSERTING NEEDLES

It's crucial that the needles sit all the way up in the needle clamp before you tighten the screws. Otherwise, you will end up with skipped and uneven stitches.

Some coverstitch machines come with a needle inserting tool called a needle holder to make this easier. A combined needle holder/threader tool can be bought separately if your machine lacks this tool. You can also use tweezers for this purpose.

1 **Raise the needles.** Turn the handwheel towards you to raise the needles to the highest position.

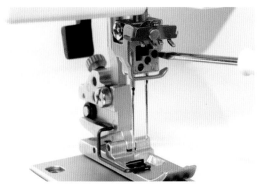

2 **Loosen the needle screw.** Then remove the needle in the bar.

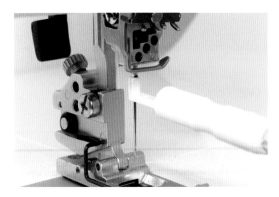

3 **Insert a new needle into the needle clamp.** Push the needle up as far as possible into the needle clamp. Make sure the screw is loose enough to allow this.

4 **Tighten the needle clamp screw.** Make sure the needle stays put and doesn't drop slightly. A needle holder will make this easier.

TIME TO CHANGE THE NEEDLE?

If you mostly hem knits on your coverstitch machine and don't sew over pins, your coverstitch needle will usually last a long time before it's time to change it. Some coverstitch/serger needles also have an extra layer of metal coating to make them even more durable.

Do note that synthetic fibres dull the needle faster than natural fibres, so if you sew a lot of activewear and swimwear on your coverstitch machine, you will need to change needles more often.

If you suddenly get skipped, uneven, or puckered stitches, try replacing the needle and see if that helps. There is no exact rule on how many sewing hours a needle will last; instead, its performance will be your guide. You can also inspect your needle and look for damage.

If your needles seem to wear down quickly, it could be a sign that the machine needs adjustment. If so, take it to a mechanic and have it inspected.

HOW TO INSPECT A NEEDLE

The easiest way to see if a needle is damaged is to compare it with an unused needle. Either use a magnifying device or your fingers and look for the following signs:

- The tip feels dull compared to the new needle

- The tip is chipped

- The needle is bent

- Wear around the needle eye

COVERSTITCH THREAD

Several types of threads can be used in a coverstitch machine, not just serger thread, but you might need to change some settings to make the thread work.

It's always very important to use quality thread. Low-quality thread can cause all sorts of problems, such as broken and skipped stitches, getting tangled into knots, or shedding, which can mess up the tension and get into the machine. Threads with more colour pigment can also affect the stitches, so a stitch sewn with black threads might look different than ones done with white threads.

If you are having problems, try switching to another brand of thread and see if that helps. Most coverstitch machines are configured for serger thread, but with some adjustments, you can use a variety of different threads in the machine.

why buying cheap low-quality serger thread makes very little sense. Do be aware that thread ages, so check older thread to see if it still holds up.

Serger thread is often made of polyester and thinner than regular sewing machine thread. Its weight is listed in either *Tex size* or *Denier (dtex)* — the most common for serger thread is *T27 (120 dtex)*. This thread type works very well on coverstitch machines.

A serger thread is cross-wound so that the thread releases from the spool easily and evenly. When sewing, the thread is pulled from the top so that the cone doesn't spin like a regular thread spool does. This is one of the reasons serger thread on spools are excellent for coverstitching, as they allow for even distribution of the thread, regardless of whether you are sewing slow or quickly.

Serger thread
Serger thread usually comes as cones, with around 2700 meters (3000 yards) of thread. That amount will last a very long time, sometimes years, which is another reason

Textured thread (woolly nylon)
This soft, stretchy, and textured thread is untwisted and spreads out when stitched, which provides excellent coverage and a soft surface that is kind to the skin. It's made of either nylon or polyester.

In the garment industry, this thread is used in the looper when hemming knits. It is generally not recommended as a needle thread, as it might get distorted.

Textured thread makes the seam extra durable and adds tension, so you might need to loosen the looper tension or increase the needle tension for the stitch to be balanced. When ironing nylon, make sure the setting is low, as nylon is more heat sensitive than polyester.

Increasing the stitch length is usually a good idea when sewing with textured thread, as the looper seam might become too bulky with a short stitch length.

Sewing machine thread

When you need particular colours or plan to use the coverstitch on woven garments, general purpose thread is your best choice. Pick a polyester thread and make sure it's from a quality brand. Sewing machine thread can be used in both the needles and the looper.

As this thread often comes on spools and not cones, you will need to use spool caps to help the thread reel freely. Adjusting the tension is usually not necessary when using regular sewing machine thread, but always sew a sample first to make sure the stitch looks balanced.

Topstitching thread

Topstitching thread, sometimes called buttonhole or jeans thread, is a thick, cord-like thread that is heavier than serger thread. Topstitching thread is primarily used in looper, as many domestic coverstitch machines are not optimised for thicker thread in the needles, but you can always test and see if it works.

As topstitching thread is thicker, you might need to loosen the tension to make the stitch balanced. Some machines recommend a different threading routine for thicker threads, so check the manual for suggestions on how to that.

Decorative threads

These come in many forms and can often be used in both the needles and looper depending on what effect you want to achieve. Easiest to sew with are decorative serger thread, such as the multicolour threads sold on spools.

You can also try using thread that is not optimised for a coverstitch machines, like silky rayon machine embroidery thread and metallics. Use a large enough needle and make sure the thread spools wind easily; use either a spool cap or thread net to achieve this. Some threads, especially thicker ones,

will only work in the looper. If the decorative thread stitch looks unbalanced, try adjusting the tension.

Clear thread

If you want your seam to be almost invisible, try using clear monofilament thread. This is usually made of nylon, but some brands make a similar thread from polyester. It looks like a fishing line but some threads are actually fairly soft and can work well on seams that will come in contact with the skin. But getting the tension right with this type of thread is not always easy.

A WORD OF ADVICE ABOUT USING SPECIALTY THREADS

Not all coverstitch machines are equipped for specialty threads. Regular sewing machine thread will usually work well, as well as woolly nylon. The rest can be somewhat of a gamble.

COVERSTITCH THREAD QUICK GUIDE

1. **SERGER THREAD.** The standard thread for coverstitching and what the machine is optimised for when it leaves the factory.

2. **WOOLLY NYLON.** Soft stretchy thread used primarily in the looper when hemming knits. Adds tension, so loosening the looper tension is often necessary.

3. **SEWING MACHINE THREAD.** Can be used in both the needles and the looper. Requires a spool cap and often a tension adjustment

4. **TOPSTITCHING THREAD.** Primarily used in the looper for decorative purposes. Usually needs less tension and can also require a different threading method.

5. **DECORATIVE THREADS.** Use thread net or spool caps to make thicker flossy decorative thread run smoother on the spools. Will often require tension adjustments, a thread net, and on some machines, a different threading method.

6. **CLEAR THREAD.** Invisible thread that is used primarily in the looper.

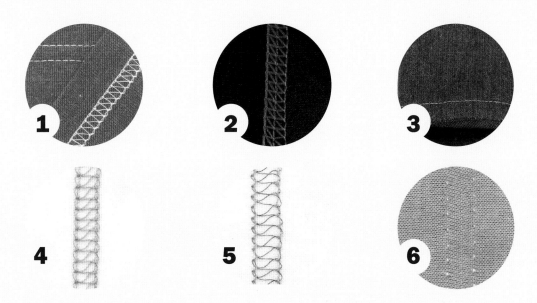

USING THREAD ACCESSORIES

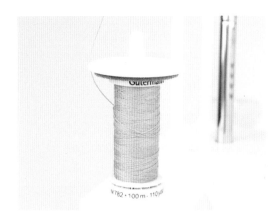

Spool cap

The spool cap adapter makes it possible to use regular sewing machine thread on the coverstitch machine. The cap is wider than the spool, which makes the thread move upwards instead of to the side as it would on a regular sewing machine. Place the thread spool on the thread pin and put the spool cap on top.

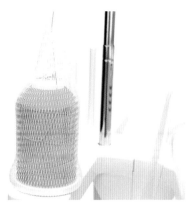

Spool net

If the thread gets stuck, slips away, or gets twisted, use a spool net. Put the net over the spool and experiment with the placement.

Make sure the net covers the bottom of the spool to prevent the thread from getting jammed between the spool and the holders. A thread net is also recommended for decorative threads, such as embroidery rayon, to make sure they run smoothly.

Cone holder

To keep the cone in place, use a cone holder. Place the cone holder over the spool rod pin and then place the thread cone over the holder, making sure it fits snugly. For extra large cones, try placing the cone holder upside down, with the wider edge facing upwards to keep the cone in place.

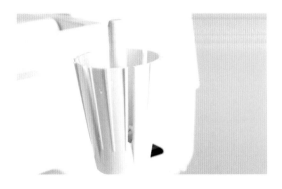

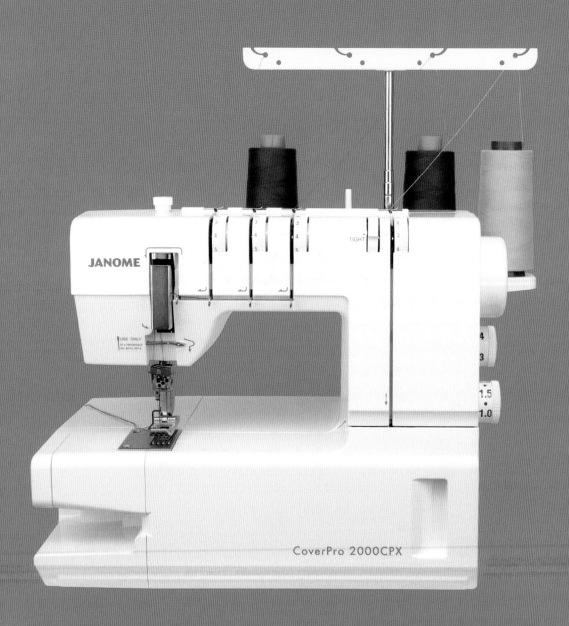

CHAPTER 3
SET-UP

THREADING THE MACHINE

A properly threaded coverstitch machine is crucial for the end result. Issues with threading are the most common cause of trouble, so one has to be meticulous when doing this step.

If you are having problems and can't see why, the first thing you should do is to rethread the machine from scratch. Threading might vary depending on the machine you have, so always consult your manual for the specifics. This step-by-step tutorial is only meant to give you an overview.

PREPARATION
- Turn the machine off
- Raise the presser foot to release the tension
- Open the looper cover

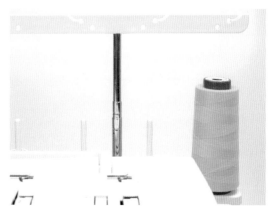

1 **Align the thread guides.** This usually means turning the handwheel to a dedicated position. Make sure the looper and thread guides are in the right position for threading. Consult your manual for this step.

2 **Start with the looper thread spool.** Make sure it sits properly and use a spool cone, a spool holder, or a spool net if needed. See *Thread accessories* on page 40 for more information on how to set up the spool cones properly.

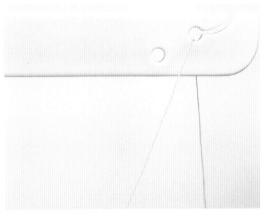 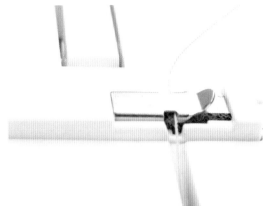

3 **Pull the thread through the thread guide on the rod.** Make sure it is placed according to the instructions and that the thread doesn't get tangled.

4 **Insert thread into the guide plate.** On some machines the thread should also be inserted into the thread guide plate, which usually sits above the tension discs.

5 **Pull the thread through the tension discs.** Hold the thread at both ends and firmly tug to make sure the thread is properly inserted between the tension discs. Pull the thread gently back and forth to make sure there is a slight resistance. This means the thread is placed correctly. Remember that the presser foot has to be up.

6 **Thread the rest of the guides in the looper area.** Follow the instructions in your manual closely. The set-up of the thread guides varies a lot depending on the machine.

7 **Release the looper.** On many machines, you need to disengage the looper to make threading easier. Consult your manual for the specifics.

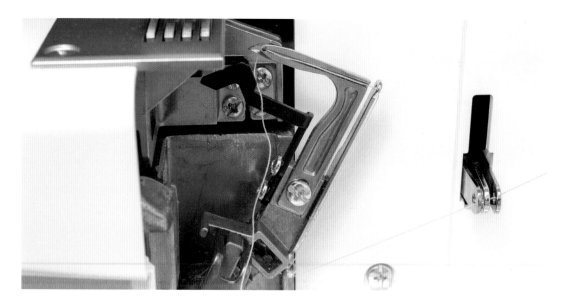

8 **Thread the looper eye.** Insert the thread in the eye and pull it through; use a pair of tweezers to make this easier. Pull about 10 cm (4 in) of thread through the looper eye and leave it there underneath the plate. On some machines, this step is automatic, which means that you don't have to pull the thread through the looper manually.

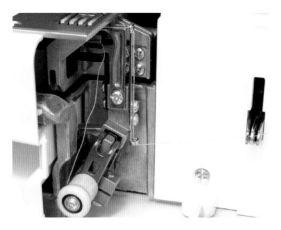

9 **Push the looper back.** It will click when it is engaged again.

10 **Thread the needle threads.** It is important that you thread each needle thread separately all the way from the thread guides to the needle eye. On many machines, it's recommended to start with the left needle and then move to the right. Check your manual for the specifics.

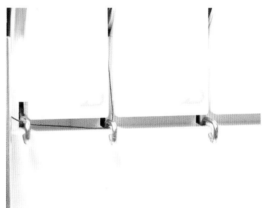

11 **Thread the guides and the tension discs.** Make sure you don't miss any guides, the thread sits firmly between the tension discs, and that the presser foot is up.

12 **Place the thread in the guides below the tension dials.** Carefully place it in the slots so that the thread doesn't slip.

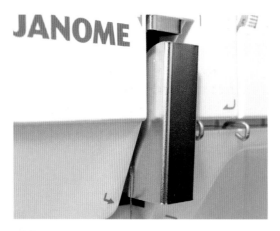

13 **Thread the take-up.** Make sure the thread sits properly in the slot behind the cover.

14 **Place the thread in the needle clamp guide.** There will a guide assigned for each needle thread.

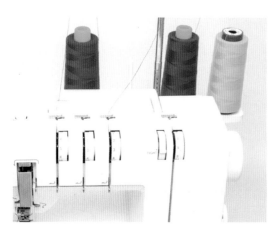

15 **Repeat for any additional needle thread.** It's important that each thread is placed in the correct assigned guide. Also make sure that threads don't get tangled together. This can easily happen, especially around the needle clamp area.

16 **Thread the needle eyes from front to back.** Lower the presser foot and use a needle threader to make it easier. Draw the thread to the left and back. The thread should be about 6–8 cm (2.5–3.5 in) long.

COVERSTITCH SETTINGS

A coverstitch machine comes with a myriad of different adjustment options, including tension, stitch length, presser foot pressure, and differential feed.

Most machines will have recommended settings listed in the manual; start with those. But sometimes adjustments are needed to improve the stitch quality, especially if you sew over thick layers or have problems with puckers, uneven feeding, or skipped stitches.

TENSION

Getting the tension right is necessary for well balanced, beautiful coverstitching. Tension is mainly regulated with the tension dials, but the thread guides, thread type, and fabric properties also affect the tension.

Having a grip on tension and being able to analyse the need for adjustments will vastly improve your end result. In general, try to avoid setting the tension too high, as this can prevent the thread from running smoothly and cause other problems too, such as puckering and tunnelling.

Tension dials

The tension dials regulate how much pressure the tension discs put on the threads. Domestic coverstitch machines usually come with recommended tension settings for both the needle and looper thread, but there will be situations where adjustments might be necessary for best result.

Tension changes required:

- When using thread other than serger threads. For instance, lower the tension when using a thicker thread. When stitching over thick layers, try loosening tension if you get unbalanced stitching or puckers.

- For lightweight fabrics, tightening the tension can help with stitch issues.

- If you are sewing over uneven layers, for instance, one needle is sewing over a single layer and the other over double layers. Then you might need to use higher tension on the needle that is sewing over the single layer, or vice versa.

Tension tip

Always adjust one dial at a time. And remember that needle and looper tension work together, so, in many instances, you can achieve the same result by either increasing the needle tension or lowering the looper tension.

Note

Thread the tension discs with the presser foot up, as this will release the discs and facilitate proper thread insertion.

DIFFERENTIAL FEED

This function controls how fast the front feed dogs will move in relation to the back feed dogs. A higher setting increases the speed and a lower setting slows the speed down. Use this setting to control puckers or stretched out fabric when hemming knits.

On many dials, there is also an "N" that stands for 'normal', which means that the front and back dogs move with the same speed. Always start with this setting, and then do the changes only if you are experiencing problems.

Differential changes required:

- Puckers on the fabric. Lowering the differential feed will prevent puckers.

- Stretched out, wavy, fabric. Increase the differential feed to prevent this.

- Sewing over thick binding. A lower differential feed setting will prevent the binding from getting scrunched up under the presser foot.

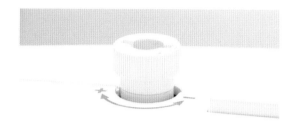

PRESSER FOOT PRESSURE

Most coverstitch machines will have a dial on top of the machine that adjusts presser foot pressure. Turn the dial counterclockwise to reduce the pressure and clockwise to increase it. Normally you can leave the presser foot dial untouched when coverstitching, but sometimes adjusting the pressure is necessary.

Pressure changes required:

- Sewing over bulky layers. Increased pressure can help prevent skipped stitches and make the fabric feed better.

- Hemming lightweight knits. A lower pressure can prevent the fabric from stretching out.

EXTRA ADJUSTMENTS

Some coverstitch machines will have additional dials that can improve the stitching. Check your manual for how to use them.

STITCH LENGTH

On most coverstitch machines, a stitch length between 3 and 4 is recommended.

Stitch length primer

- In general, a longer stitch length is more beneficial than a shorter one when it comes to coverstitching.

- Increasing the length can prevent skipped stitches, keep ridges from forming between the stitch rows, and make the fabric feed easier, which is especially helpful when stitching over bulky layers.

- When sewing elastic and binding, increasing the stitch length will also be helpful as the stitches will contract and become smaller once sewn.

- Longer stitches will make the seam less stretchy. Try a sample to see if the seam will stretch out enough on your garment.

CHAPTER 4
SEAMS

COVERSTITCH SEAMS

Coverstitch seams are primarily used for hemming, topstitching, and decorative purposes. The appeal of the coverstitch for home sewists is primarily its ability to provide a highly elastic, durable, and visually pleasing hemming stitch. But the coverstitch and chainstitch seams can be used for lots of other finishings too.

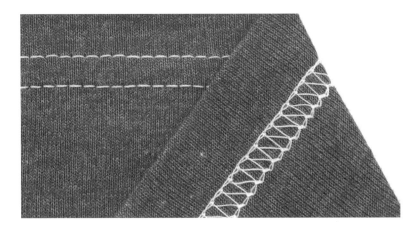

What is a coverstitch seam?

A coverstitch is an elastic seam formed by two or more needles and one looper. On the front, the stitches are straight and on the reverse side, a grid pattern is formed by the looper thread crossing back and forth between the needle threads.

This elastic and durable stitch is perfect for both hemming and topstitching, especially on knits. But the stitch can also be used in wovens, for instance, when sewing belt loops. As the name implies, the reverse side of a coverstitch seam provides excellent coverage that can also be used on the right side for decorative stitching

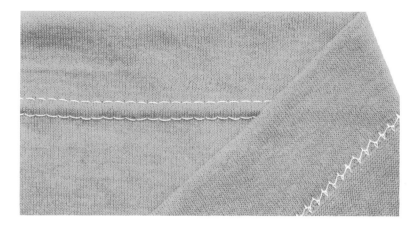

The difference between a
twin-needle and coverstitch seam

Using a twin needle on a regular sewing machine is a practical way to create an elastic and neat hem on knits. On the right side it looks quite similar to a narrow 2-needle coverstitch seam, but on the reverse side, there is a zigzag stitch instead of a looper grid.

The twin-needle is generally slightly less elastic than a coverstitch seam, and can sometimes break when stretched to its limit. Also, the twin-needle stitch is more prone to tunnelling, where a ridge is formed between the rows of stitches.

That said, tunnelling can be an issue on coverstitch seams as well, especially when sewing on thin, very stretchy fabrics.

The difference between serger and coverstitch seams

Both sergers and coverstitch machines sew stitches that form loops and they are technically very similar, which is why you can buy machines that both serge seams and coverstitch. But you will not be able to sew a straight stitch and folded hem with a regular, stand-alone serger.

COVERSTITCH SEAMS

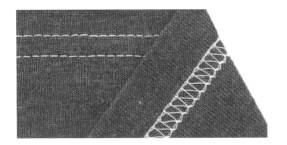

WIDE 2-NEEDLE COVERSTITCH

The professional-standard stitch for hemming knit fabrics. A 2-needle, 3-thread coverstitch that has a high amount of stretch. Can be used for hemming, topstitching, neckline binding, belt loops, and decorative seams. Also called bottom coverstitch, this stitch is formed by two needle threads passing through the fabric and intertwining with the looper thread.

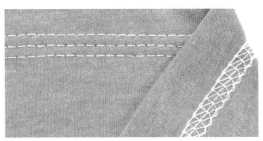

TRIPLE 3-NEEDLE COVERSTITCH

A decorative and durable coverstitch with three parallel rows of stitching. This 4-thread durable coverstitch seam can be used for hemming, decorative stitching, elastic, and to create mock flatlock seams. As the looper thread is inter-looped between all the needle threads, the reverse side provides excellent coverage and can be used as a decorative stitch too.

NARROW 2-NEEDLE COVERSTITCH

A narrow version of the regular coverstitch hem. This 2-needle, 3-thread coverstitch can be used for hemming, binding, and topstitching and is a popular choice for children's clothes and underwear. Available on 3-needle coverstitch machines.

1-NEEDLE CHAINSTITCH

A straight chainstitch seam that uses one needle and one looper thread. Use for binding, hemming, and topstitching (perfect for jeans). The chainstitch has more stretch than a regular straight seam and is formed by one needle thread being interlooped with one looper thread that is set on the underside of the seam.

SPECIALTY STITCHES

These stitches are only available on specialty machines such as serger/coverstitch combo machines and top-coverstitch machines. These machines usually have slots for five thread spools or more and you might need to do additional adjustments in order to sew these speciality stitches.

3-NEEDLE TOP-COVERSTITCH

3-needle, 1-top-cover, and 1-looper double faced coverstitch seam. This creates a decorative and elastic five-thread stitch both on the right and reverse side of the fabric. Use for hems, topstitching, flat joining seams, and attaching elastic and bindings. Available on top-coverstitch machines.

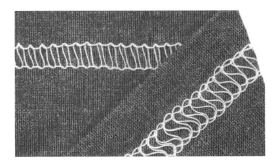

2-NEEDLE TOP-COVERSTITCH

A 2-needle, 1-top-cover, and 1-looper double face coverstitch seam. This decorative 4-thread stitch can be used for hems, topstitching, flat joining seams, and attaching elastic and bindings. Perfect for children's clothes and underwear. Available on top-coverstitch machines.

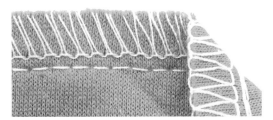

SAFETY STITCH

This sturdy seam combines a straight chain-stitch seam with an overedge stitch. Popular in the garment industry, this seam both sews a straight seam and overcasts the fabric simultaneously, which saves a lot of time. The safety stitch is perfect for making jeans and other projects where durability is important. Available on serger/coverstitch combination machines.

COVERSTITCH TENSION GUIDE

Getting the stitch tension balanced can be a challenge and is often a case of trial and error. However using different colour threads, a magnifying device, and a methodical approach where you don't change several settings at once will make this process easier.

2-NEEDLE COVERSTITCH

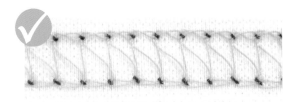

Balanced tension

- The looper thread (yellow) forms even loops on the reverse side and the needle threads are small, firm loops.

- The two rows of stitches on the top side are straight and even with no puckers.

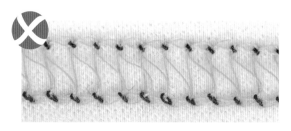

Needle tension too loose (red thread)/ looper too tight

- The needle threads form larger loops on the reverse side (shown).

- One or both rows of straight stitches on the top side are uneven and loose.

- There are visible gaps in the loops.

Solution:

- Increase the needle thread tension on one or both needles.

- Try loosening the looper thread tension.

Needle tension too tight (green thread)/looper too loose

- The needle thread loops pull the looper thread too tightly, forming uneven loops.

- Puckers on the fabric.

- The needle thread forms very tiny knots.

Solution

- Loosen the needle thread tension.

- Tighten the looper thread tension (sometimes a combination of both adjustments works best).

3-NEEDLE COVERSTITCH

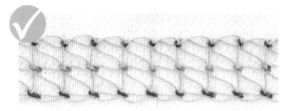

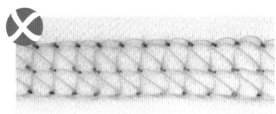

Balanced tension

- The needle thread should be visible only as small "knots" on the reverse side, not large loops (shown)

- All three rows of straight stitches are even.

- The looper thread forms two rows of squares with diagonal lines inside.

Needle tension too tight/ looper too loose

- The needle thread loops pull the looper thread too tightly, forming uneven loops.

- The needle thread forms very tiny knots.

Solution:

- Loosen the needle thread tension.

- Tighten the looper thread tension.

- Try a combination of both looper and needle adjustments.

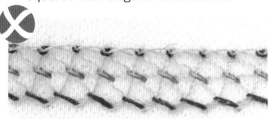

Needle tension too loose (red and green thread)/looper tension too tight

- The needle threads form larger, uneven loops on the reverse side (shown).

- One or several stitch rows on the top side are irregular.

- The looper thread formation is uneven.

Solution:

- Increase the needle thread tension on one or both needles (only on the rows that look uneven).

- Try loosening the looper thread tension.

- Use a combination of both adjustments.

CHAINSTITCH

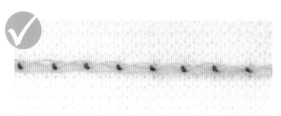

Balanced tension

- The looper thread should form loops and the needle thread should be visible only as small knots on the reverse side, There should be no large loops.

- A straight, even seam on the top side with no puckers.

Needle tension too tight/ looper too loose

- Puckers on the fabric.

- The needle thread forms very tiny knots.

Solution:

- Loosen the needle thread tension or tighten the looper thread tension to correct it.

Needle tension too loose/ looper tension too hard

- The straight stitch on the top side is uneven and loose.

- The needle thread forms larger loops on the wrong side of the fabric.

Solution:

- Increase the needle thread tension or loosen the looper thread tension.

TROUBLESHOOTING GUIDE

A lot of things can go wrong when coverstitching, especially if the machine has not been set up properly. Certain fabrics also provide challenges that can result in wonky stitching and other problems. Here is a guide with solutions to common coverstitch issues.

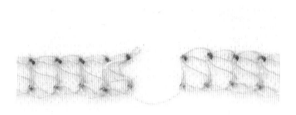

SKIPPED STITCHES

A skipped stitch happens when a loop is not formed or picked up. On coverstitch machines, this is a fairly common problem especially when sewing on knits.

- Check that the machine is threaded properly.
- Make sure you are using the correct needles.
- Try switching to a brand new needle.
- Use a ballpoint needle for knits.
- Insert the needle correctly, all the way up in the bar.
- Increase the stitch length.
- Increase the presser foot pressure.
- Try another needle size.
- Adjust the tension.
- Don't pull the fabric to the back when coverstitching, just gently guide it with your hands.

TUNNELLING

When a tunnel (ridge) is formed between the straight stitch rows. Common on lightweight knits, especially if the left needle only sews a single layer of fabric when hemming.

- Increase the stitch length.
- Lower the presser foot pressure.
- Lower the looper tension.
- Lower the differential feed.
- Sew over removable stabilising material, such as double-sided wonder tape or a water-soluble non-woven.
- Make sure all the needles sew over both layers of the fabric.

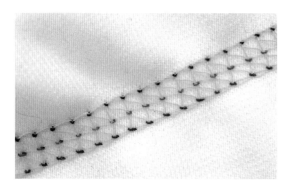

PUCKERING

Puckering means that the seam gathers up, causing wrinkles. It is more common on lightweight fabrics and can appear on both knits and wovens.

- Decrease the differential feed (set it to a lower number).
- Loosen the needle tension and/ or tighten the looper tension.
- Reduce the presser foot pressure.

WAVY FABRIC

Excessive stretching can happen when coverstitching over knit fabrics or woven fabrics cut on the bias. Luckily, this problem is usually easy to fix on a coverstitch machine

- Make sure you don't pull the fabric when sewing, just guide it gently.

- Use a higher differential feed setting.
- Increase the stitch length.
- Decrease the presser foot pressure.
- If the above suggestions don't help, stabilise the hem with fusible interfacing or use a water-soluble double-sided tape.

DRAGLINES

This happens when the upper and lower layer of the fabric feeds unevenly during hemming, causing diagonal draglines. Curved seams, in particular, are prone to this happening.

- Lighten the presser foot pressure.
- Adjust the differential feed—usually a lower setting can help.
- Use a sharp, pointed object, such as an awl, to gently push the upper layer towards the presser foot.
- Baste or use evenly spaced pins to make sure that each section is evenly fed. Water-soluble basting glue or regular stick glue can also help keep the fabric layers in check.

FABRIC DOESN'T FEED

On a coverstitch, the fabric should feed evenly and easily, without having to pull the fabric. If the fabric bunches up under the presser foot, it means that something is wrong.

- Increase the stitch length.
- Adjust the presser foot pressure (increasing is usually better).
- When sewing over thick layers, try increasing the speed.
- Have a mechanic check that the feed dogs are working properly.

THREAD BREAKS

A thread that breaks is actually quite rare on most domestic coverstitch machines, but it can happen, especially if the thread is getting stuck somewhere and doesn't feed properly.

- Check that the thread isn't tangled up in a thread guide.
- Make sure the thread reels easily from the spool. If the thread gets jammed or knotted, use the accessories described in the thread chapter on page 40.
- Loosen the tension.
- Use high-quality thread.
- Make sure the needle is inserted correctly.
- Change needles.

COVERSTITCH SEAM UNRAVELS

If the ends of the coverstitch seam aren't secured correctly or if the loops are not formed properly, unravelling coverstitch seams will occur, either immediately or after a few wears.

- Secure the seam correctly (see *How to secure coverstitch* seams on pages 76–80).
- Make sure the loops are formed properly (see *Skipped stitches* on page 61).

"Coverstitching is not that hard"

"I would say that coverstitching is pretty straightforward". Sewing teacher and machine expert Kicci Johansson is quite surprised to hear that some people find the coverstitch machine a struggle to use.

She makes the argument that if the threading is done correctly and the right kind of needles are used, the result should be satisfactory.

But still, things do happen and here Kicci gives her best tips on how to avoid them.

What are the most common causes of skipped stitches?

There are several reasons why this happens. One thing I see in my classes is that people have a tendency to pull the fabric when they are coverstitching. I understand why they do it because that is how we do it on a regular sewing machine. But doing that on a coverstitch machines messes up the feeding of the fabric and skipped stitches can be the result of this pulling.

Another reason is that they are using a faulty needle, so I always recommend that you start by switching your needles and see if that helps.

And the third reason for skipped stitches is that the thread is not properly placed in the tension discs. You need to make sure the thread sits all the way in.

But occasionally the machine can be faulty too, right? So what are common problems with a coverstitch machine?

First of all, I want to say that we don't get many repair requests on coverstitch machines, they are usually very sturdy, hardly ever break and will last many, many years.

But, of course, sometimes there are problems with the actual machine. I would say that the most common issue is that the feed dogs are not feeding the fabric properly, and that is something a mechanic can fix.

Also, another problem that I have encountered is that the stitch length mechanics stop working, which means that you can no longer adjust the stitch length, even though you can move the knob.

Sewing over bulky layers is not always easy with a coverstitch machine. What are your best tips?

People often need to sew faster. Yes, I really mean that. I see so many people slowing down when they encounter bulky layers, but they need to do the opposite. A higher speed will make it easier for the machine to properly sew over thick seams and such, and it will prevent skipped stitches too.

Try adjusting the presser foot pressure too, it should generally be increased when sewing over thicker layers. That said, keep in mind that you are using a domestic coverstitch machine and not an industrial one. It is not really built for sewing over thick layers, that is just how it is.

Sometimes, a tunnel is formed between the stitches when sewing a 2-needle coverstitch. What causes that?

Usually, the stitch length is too short. Switch to the longest setting and see if that helps. Another reason for getting those ridges is that the looper tension is too tight, so try loosening it a little.

Another problem is that the fabric is not feeding properly and it gets bunched up under the presser foot. What can we do about that?

It means that feed dogs are not properly feeding the fabric. My best solution is to increase the stitch length. A short stitch length will make it harder to feed fabric and the feed dogs will eat up the fabric, so to speak.

If that doesn't help I would consult a mechanic to make sure there is nothing wrong with the machine.

QUICK GUIDE: **COVERSTITCH MACHINE STITCHES**

STITCH	LOOK	USE	PROPERTIES
WIDE 2-NEEDLE COVERSTITCH		• Hemming • Belt loops • Topstitching • Neckband • Binding • Elastic	• Great stretch • Durable • Professional finish • Keeps the knit from stretching out when sewing
NARROW 2-NEEDLE COVERSTITCH		• Hemming • Topstitching • Neckband • Binding • Pintucks	• Great stretch • Durable • Professional finish • Keeps the knit from stretching out when sewing
TRIPLE 3-NEEDLE COVERSTITCH		• Hemming • Decorative stitches • Topstitching • Mock flatlock • Binding	• Great coverage • Durable • Professional finish • Keeps the knit from stretching out when sewing
1-NEEDLE CHAINSTITCH		• Topstitching • Neckband • Binding • Hemming jeans • Basting • Jeans making	• Great stretch • Unravels if not secured • Professional finish
3-NEEDLE TOP COVERSTITCH		• Hemming • Decorative stitches • To mimic ready-to-wear activewear • Mock flatlock • Elastic	• Great coverage • Looks great on both sides • Professional finish • Keeps the knit from stretching out when sewing
2-NEEDLE TOP COVERSTITCH		• Hemming • Decorative stitches • To mimic ready-to-wear activewear • Mock flatlock • Elastic	• Professional finish • Keeps the knit from stretching out when sewing • Great coverage • Non-bulky

CHAPTER 5

SEWING

HEMMING: IN THE ROUND

Hemming after the side seams are sewn creates a neat finish. On wider pieces, this is very easy, but hemming smaller tubes, such as leg openings and sleeves, can be tricky, as most cover-stitch machines don't have a free arm. But with practice, it is certainly doable, even on children's clothes.

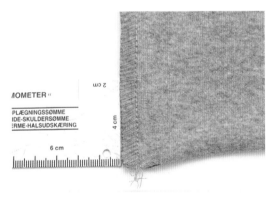

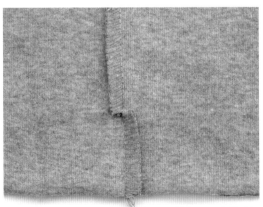

1 **Prepare for hemming.** Make sure the edges of the fabric are evenly cut. Measure the width of the hem to prepare for clipping.

2 **Clip the seam allowance.** If your seam is secure enough, clip the side seams at the fold and lay the clipped seam in the opposite direction to remove bulk when hemming.

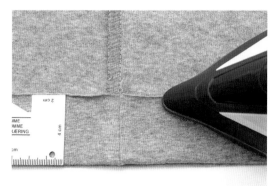

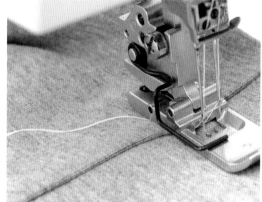

3 **Fold the hem.** On materials that can take a little heat, ironing the fold is recommended as it makes hemming easier. With practice, you'll be able to hem using just your fingers to keep the fold even. But you can also hand-baste the hem using large stitches.

4 **Insert the fabric.** Lift the presser foot and move the needles to the highest position. Insert the garment under the presser foot and needles.

TIP: Start stitching just after a seam, preferably on the inner or back side of the garment, as bulk can be tricky for the machine to handle during the first few stitches.

5 **Start stitching.** Make sure you guide the tube evenly with your hands, without pulling the fabric.

6 **Finish the seam.** Overlap the end and beginning for around 1.5 cm (3/5 in).

7 **Lift the presser foot and release the threads.** You cannot backstitch on a coverstitch machine, so the end threads have to be secured. See pages 76–80 for methods that will secure the seams.

8 **Remove the fabric.** Pinch the seam as you remove the garment to avoid the threads unravelling if you haven't secured the seam yet. Make sure the thread strands are around 10 cm (4 in) long.

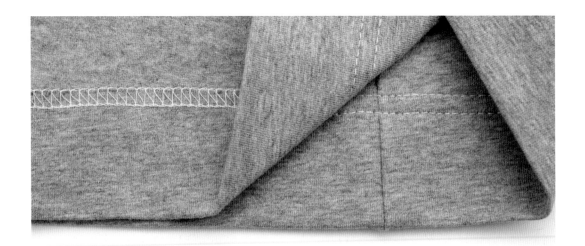

9 **The finished hem.** A coverstitch machine will achieve a very professional-looking hem. It also has excellent stretch and recovery compared with most sewing machine stitches. For a neat finish, sew close to the edge of the fabric so that the seam covers the edge.

HEMMING: FLAT ASSEMBLY

Use this method when you are sewing flat pieces, such as hemming a sleeve before sewing the side seam. Sewing in the flat is the easiest way to coverstitch hems, especially if you are sewing narrow pieces. When the hemming is done, sew the side seam to close the garment.

This method is very common in the garment industry, and can also be used when hemming several pieces at once. After you have hemmed one piece, insert the next one until you have hemmed all the flat pieces.

1 **Fold the hem.** On materials that can take a little heat, ironing the fold is recommended as it makes hemming easier.

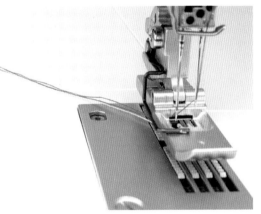

2 **Prepare the machine.** Lift the presser foot. Raise the needles to the highest position. Pull all threads back and to the left. The strands should be about 10 cm (4 in) long.

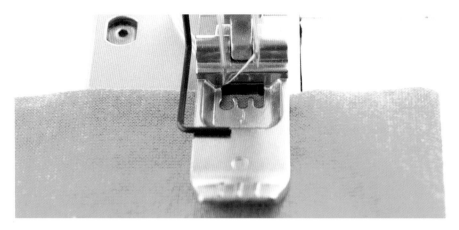

3 **Insert the fabric.** Place the fabric underneath the presser foot. Make sure the needles will catch the fabric on the first stitch. Lower the presser foot and start sewing.

TIP: If you are experiencing problems in the beginning, try sewing the first 2–3 stitches using the handwheel, instead of the foot pedal.

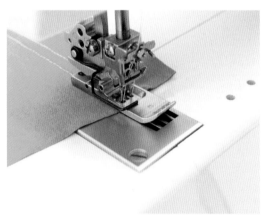

4 **Start sewing slowly.** But don't be afraid to increase the speed after the first few stitches. Never pull or stretch the fabric during stitching. Just gently guide it with your hands to make sure the seam is straight.

5 **Stop just before the edge of the fabric.** Lift the presser foot and raise the needles. This will release the threads on most machines, but check the manual for the specifics on your machine.

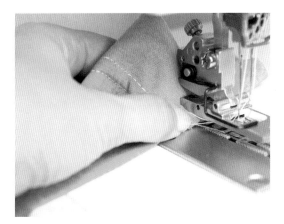

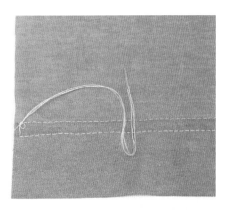

6 **Remove the fabric.** Pinch the seam between your fingers and pull the fabric away from the presser foot. Make sure the thread strands are around 10 cm (4 in) long.

7 **Secure the threads.** Knot all three threads or use your preferred method for securing a seam (see pages 76–80).

8 **Stitch the side seam.** Make sure the seam catches the coverstitch hem stitches so that the hem stitching won't unravel.

9 **The finished piece.** To keep the seam allowance in place, sew a vertical line of tacking stitches over the seam allowance. Do this from the right side.

SECURING THE SEAMS

You cannot backstitch on a coverstitch machine, and if the ends are not secured, the seam will unravel quickly. Fortunately, there are many ways to finish and secure a coverstitch seam, and it can also vary depending on the machine.

Here is an overview of the most common methods. You only need to secure the ends of a seam.

The beginning of the seam is automatically secured because the first stitch is fastened by the subsequent stitches. On some machines, there is also a built-in function to secure the seams.

THE PULL METHOD
This method both secures and pulls the needle threads to the reverse side in one movement. Some machines can do this automatically, but on most, you have to do this by hand.

1 **Prepare for securing.** Close the seam by sewing over the beginning stitches for a few centimetres (an inch or less). Place the thread strands vertically before closing the seam to prevent the threads from getting caught in the seam.

2 **Move the needles to the highest position.** Use the handwheel. The needles need to be high up for this method to work properly. Then lift the presser foot.

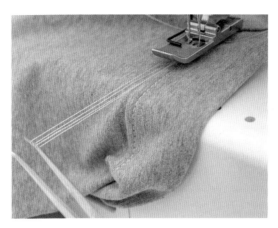

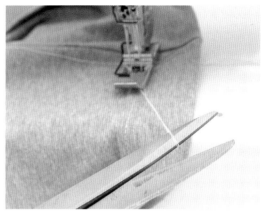

3 **Pull the threads.** Use a crochet hook, tweezers, or some other narrow tool, and pull the needle threads towards you. Make the loops around 4–5 cm (2 in) long.

4 **Clip the thread loops.** Insert a pair of scissors in the middle of the loops and cut.

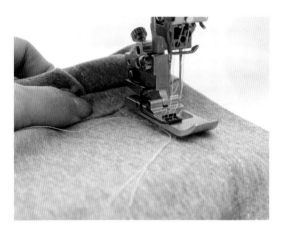

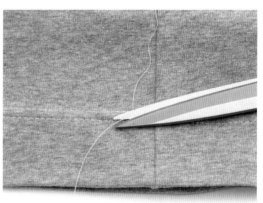

5 **Pinch and pull the fabric.** Grab the fabric behind the presser foot and pinch the seam with your fingers; this will prevent tunnelling when the thread is pulled. Then pull it firmly and diagonally to the back. This moves the needle threads to the reverse side and secures the stitch.

6 **Cut the beginning needle threads.** Now the hem is secured. This method is perfect when sewing in the round, but can also be used for flat assembly.

SECURE WITH A SCRAP

This method is a quick way to finish the seam when sewing flat pieces but is only recommended if you will close the edges afterwards with a secure seam, such as an overlock seam.

1 **Insert a scrap.** Stop sewing at the end of your garment fabric. Insert a piece of scrap fabric underneath the presser foot.

2 **Sew on the scrap.** Sew for 5 cm (2 in) and release the threads.

3 **Cut the scrap.** Around 1.5–2.5 cm (3/5 in–1 in) of the scrap should be left attached to the garment seam. Remove the excess scrap when closing the seam. If you use a serger, just cut away the scrap with the serger knife.

Tips for successful coverstitching

- Use the right needles and switch to fresh ones if you are having problems

- Start with a clean machine

- Thread the machine correctly (check your manual)

- Never thread the machine with the presser foot down

- Don't pull the fabric when coverstitching

- Try to reduce bulk when possible

- Experiment with the presser foot pressure, stitch length and differential feed

- Do samples to test the settings

- Write down your best settings for each project

- Use good-quality thread and adjust the tension when using novelty thread

- Use a seam guide to help you stitch straighter

- Sew with confidence, you can do this!

HOW TO REMOVE A SEAM

1. UNSECURED SEAM

A regular coverstitch seam is very easy to remove, all you have to do is open the looper thread and pull the thread. This will also release the needle threads.

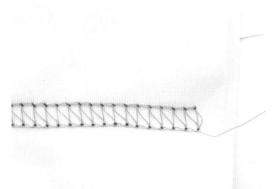

1   **Don't secure the threads.** Just release the threads and cut them so you have a 10 cm (4 in) long tail.

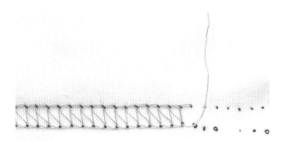

2   **Grab the looper thread.** Pull the thread towards the start of the stitch.

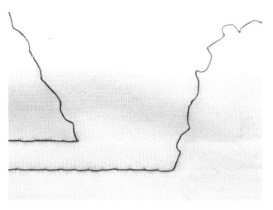

3   **Remove the needle threads.** Flip the garment and remove the needle threads with your fingers.

2. SECURED SEAM

If the looper and needle threads are tied into a knot, unpicking a seam will require a little more effort. But it's still easy to do.

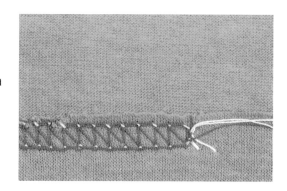

1 **Unpick the looper thread.** Cut the knot open with a small pair of scissors. Insert a needle or an awl inside the looper thread. Lift and wiggle to release the threads from the needle loops. It might take a few tries before all the threads are released.

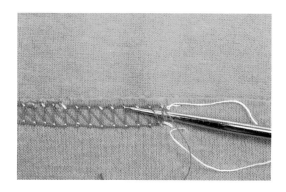

2 **Release the looper threads.** Once the needle and looper thread are separated you can pull the looper thread.

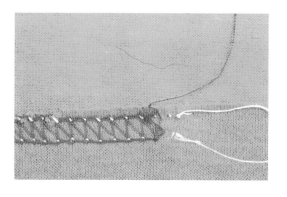

3 **Remove the threads.** Pull the looper thread towards the start of the stitching. Then flip the garment and remove the needle threads.

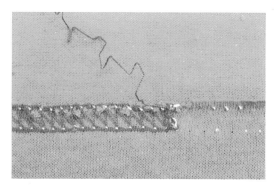

STITCHED DOWN SEAMS: STRADDLE POSITION

A popular ready-to-wear finish is to let the coverstitch straddle the seamline. Use this method when stitching down ribbing on necklines and cuffs to create a professional finish on your garment.

As you will be stitching through uneven layers (single layer vs. three layers of fabric), an adjustment of the needle tensions might be necessary. Start with a sample to check that the seam looks balanced on the reverse side and change tension if needed.

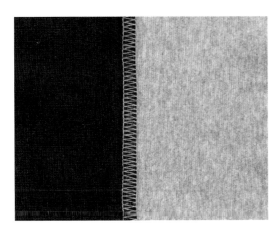
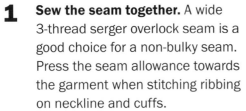

1 **Sew the seam together.** A wide 3-thread serger overlock seam is a good choice for a non-bulky seam. Press the seam allowance towards the garment when stitching ribbing on neckline and cuffs.

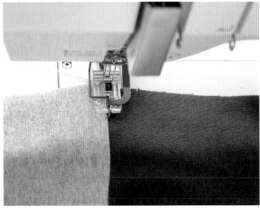

2 **Prepare for sewing.** Lift the presser foot and insert the fabric. Make sure that the mid-point of the presser foot aligns with the ditch of the seamline. A presser foot with a centre guide makes it easier but is not necessary.

3 **Start stitching.** If you don't have a centre guide presser foot, most coverstitch presser feet will have a mid-point/middle needle marking on the sole that can be used as a guide to make sure the stitch is even.

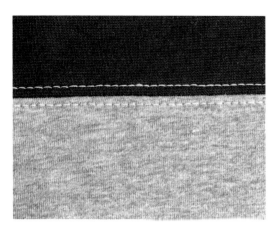

4 **Right side.** By using a coverstitch machine, you'll achieve perfectly parallel stitching that will also keep the seam allowance down.

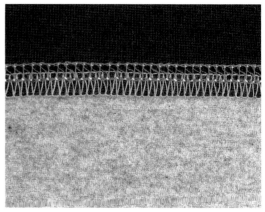

5 **Reverse side.** As the seam allowance is pressed in one direction, the looper thread will only partly cover the seam allowance.

STITCHED DOWN SEAMS: OVER THE SEAM ALLOWANCE

This method creates a beautiful finish that will keep the seam allowance in place and strengthen the durability of the seam. It is commonly used on necklines and active-wear, but is not without a few challenges, as you'll be sewing over three layers of fabric, which can result in uneven feeding and skipped stitches.

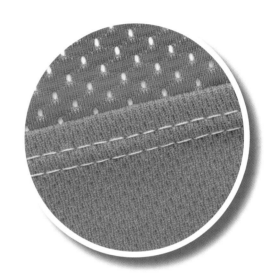

Best used for thinner fabrics. Always make samples to make sure that the tension and presser foot pressure are adjusted correctly.

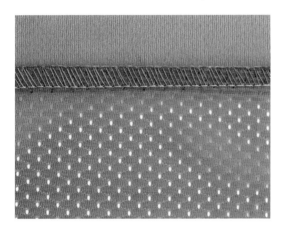

1 **Sew the seam together.** A wide 3-thread serger overlock seam with longer stitch length is a good choice for a non-bulky seam. A narrow zigzag stitch is another good option.

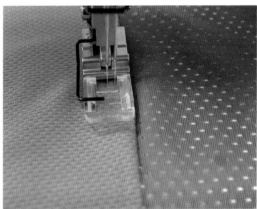

2 **Stitch along the seam.** Sew over the seam allowance, using either the outside or inner right edge on the presser foot as your guide.

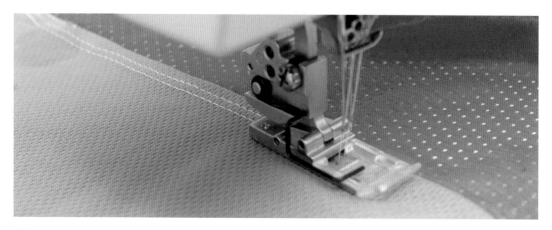

3 **Make sure both rows catch the seam allowance.**
If the fabric doesn't feed properly, increase the presser foot pressure and/or use a longer stitch length.

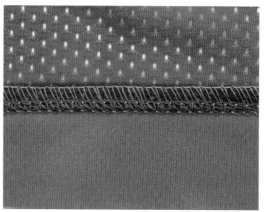

4 **Right side.** The rows of stitching will keep the seam allowance in place.

TIP: You can also use a chainstitch for a single row of stitching.

5 **Reverse side.** The looper thread will enclose the seam allowance.

REVERSE COVERSTITCHING

The reverse side of the 3-needle coverstitch has a decorative effect that can also be used on the right side of the garment. However, this is not always an easy seam to succeed with as the bulky seam increases the risk for skipped stitches and uneven feeding.

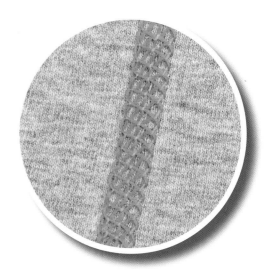

TIPS FOR REVERSE COVERSTITCHING

- Woolly nylon in the lower looper gives the seam better coverage
- Reverse coverstitching works best on thin and supple fabrics
- Increase the presser foot pressure when sewing over bulky seams
- Increase the stitch length for better feeding of the seam

- Experiment with using different needle tensions, as not all needles will sew over the same number of layers
- Always do a sample first to test the settings
- Use 90/14-size needles to prevent skipped stitches when sewing over thicker layers if your fabric can handle them (always do a sample first)

METHOD 1:
SEAMS PRESSED OPEN

This method is the least bulky and will generally yield the best result when doing reverse coverstitching. The seam allowance is pressed open and then stitched over using a 3-needle coverstitch.

1 **Sew the seam.** Use a narrow zigzag stitch, a straight stitch, or a chainstitch. The seam allowance should be around 0.6 cm (1/4 in) or slightly less. Open up the seam, so that it lies flat.

2 **Press the seam apart.** If the fabric can be ironed, use a low heat setting and press open the seam allowance.

3 **Insert the fabric.** Place the fabric wrong side up underneath the presser foot. Align the seam so that the middle needle hits the groove.

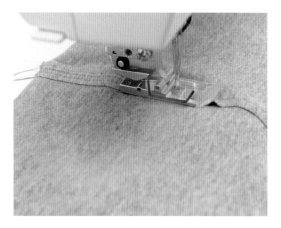

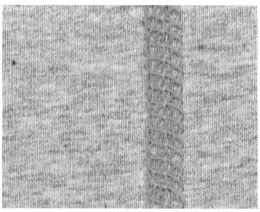

4 **Sew over the seam using the 3-needle coverstitch.** There will be three rows of straight stitches on the wrong side of the fabric and the looper thread will be on the right side.

5 **The finished seam on the right side.** In this example, a woolly nylon is used in the looper for a more decorative coverage.

METHOD 2:
OVER AN OVERLOCKED SEAM

This method is popular for stitching down seams. It will create a somewhat bulky seam so this method is generally not recommended for thicker fabrics.

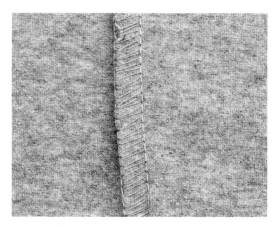

1 **Stitch the seam.** Use a wide 3-thread overlock with regular thread or a sewing machine stretch overlock seam. It's important to have a seam that is not bulky but wide enough for the coverstitch to properly grip the seam with the feed dogs.

2 **Prepare for stitching.** Experiment with folding the seam allowance to the right or left to see which side that gives the feed dogs on your machine the best grip.

3 **Sew over the seam using the 3-needle coverstitch.** Here the middle needle is aligned with the seam line, but you can experiment with the needle positions to see which one works best. Gently pull the fabric around the seam outwards so that the seam will be flat when stitched over.

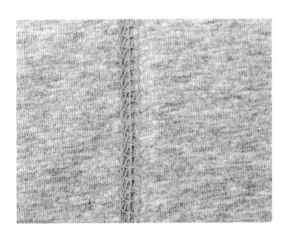

4 **The finished seam.** In this example, a woolly nylon thread is used in the looper and regular thread in the needles.

"There are no shortcuts with a coverstitch machine"

"Having patience is very important when learning to use a coverstitch machine". Fabric shop owner and sewing machine dealer Yvonne Karlsson thinks that the right mindset is crucial for a new cover-stitch user and that skipping the basics can have a detrimental effect on the end result, which is why practice is important.

What are some common beginner issues that you see?
Not taking the time to learn the machine properly. Not knowing what a looper is or how to thread the machine the right way. There are many things to keep track of when using a coverstitch machine, which is why it's so important to set aside time to learn and test in the beginning. Otherwise it's easy to get disappointed with the machine.

With a coverstitch machine there are no shortcuts, and I think you need to be interested in learning about sewing machines in order to fully master it.

Share your best buyer's advice
Buy your machine at a place that will help you get started and where you can come back and get help. I'm not a fan of online sewing machine sales.

Also, I've found that combination machines that require cumbersome switching back and forth often don't perform as well as stand-alone machines do—especially those at a lower price range.

It's hard to configure a machine to do serging and coverstitching equally well. That said, I'm a big fan of the BabyLock combination machines; they are fantastic, but their set-up is very different compared with lower-end combination machines.

95

"SET ASIDE TIME TO LEARN AND TEST THINGS IN THE BEGINNING"

What is your advice to someone who is choosing between a top-cover or a regular coverstitch machine?

If you have no prior experience with coverstitch machines, my advice would be to start with a regular coverstitch machine, just to learn the basics and get familiar. You can do almost everything with a regular machine, the top-cover is more of an icing on the cake and not a necessity.

The reason for this advice is that the fifth thread in the looper adds an extra challenge, even for experienced users. When I got my Brother top-cover machine, it took me over a month of practice before I even began talking about the fact that I owned one!

But if you still want to begin with a top-cover machine, my advice is to start with the regular 4-thread set-up and learn that way. And once you are comfortable with the regular coverstitch functions, you can start experimenting with the fifth thread.

YVONNE'S GUIDE TO TROUBLESHOOTING

- **Check the needles.** Make sure that you are using the right needles and that they sit properly all the way up in the needle clamp—just a fraction of a millimetre can throw things off.

- **Check the threading.** It only takes one thread to throw the entire seam off.

- **Thread with the presser foot up**. This will release the tension discs and allow the thread to be correctly placed between discs, which will result in the correct tension.

- **Start over.** If you can't figure out what's wrong, re-thread all threads. Make sure you do it correctly according to the instructions for your machine. This will solve most problems!

YVONNE KARLSSON
SEWING VENDOR

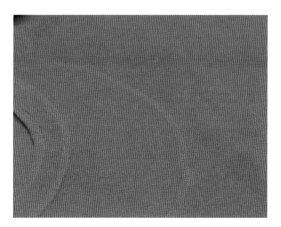

CHAPTER 6
PROJECTS

ATTACHING STRETCH LACE

A coverstitch is excellent for attaching stretch lace on a garment. It provides great stretch and the stitch will also be very discreet if you use matching thread in the needles. This method describes how to attach stretch lace in the round.

>> **SUPPLIES**

- A narrow or wide 2-needle stitch
- Serger thread for the needles
- Serger thread or woolly nylon in the looper
- Sewing needle and thread or a sewing machine for basting

1 **Cut the lace.** If sewing curves, such as arm openings, the lace should be a little shorter than the garment. On waistbands and other straighter areas, cut the lace the same length, or just slightly shorter.

2 **Close the stretch lace.** Stitch the lace together with a narrow zigzag stitch to create a loop.

3 **Pin the lace to the right side of the garment.** Align the seam of the lace with a seam of the garment. Let the lace overlap the fabric about 0.4-0.6 cm (around ¼ in).

4 **Machine or hand baste the lace.** Use a long machine basting stitch to attach the lace. An edge presser foot will make this easier. If attaching the lace to rounded areas, such as necklines and arm openings, stretch the lace to make sure it lies flat.

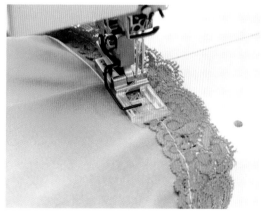

5 **The basted lace.** After the coverstitching is done, the basting stitches will be removed.

6 **Stitch the lace.** Use the pattern of the lace and the edge of the garment fabric as guides to ensure that the stitch is even. You can also use a hemming guide for this purpose.

TIP: A clear presser foot can make it easier to stitch the lace evenly.

7   **Overlap the stitch.** Sew over the start of the seam for about 2.5 cm (1 in) and then secure the stitch using your preferred method.

8   **Remove the basting thread.** Pull carefully so that you don't damage the coverstitching.

9   **The finished lace.** Notice how the looper stitch covers the edge of the garment. This might require a little practice in order to gauge the stitch correctly.

BONUS TIP: If the round areas are stretched out and don't recover, try to increase the differential feed on those areas and then return to a regular setting on the more stable areas.

FOLD-OVER ELASTIC

You can use a coverstitch machine to attach fold-over elastic. But this method will only work for a flat assembly, so one seam needs to be left open and not closed until after the elastic is attached.

SUPPLIES

- A narrow or wide 2-needle stitch
- Serger thread for the needles
- Serger thread or woolly nylon in the looper
- Sewing needle and thread or a sewing machine for basting

PREPARATION

Fold-over elastic needs to be stretched out when attached, especially in the curves. So, in general, the elastic should be shorter than your finished garment, unless the garment is very tight-fitting to begin with. Around 85% to 95% of the garment measurement is a good starting point. But you can also stretch out the elastic as you sew, in which case you don't have to measure beforehand.

You also need to add around 5 cm (2 in) at the start and finish of the fold-over elastic, to give the coverstitch seam enough margins and prevent unravelling.

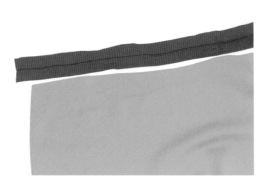

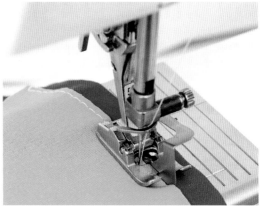

1 **Prepare for basting.** Leave one seam open, such as the side seam or shoulder seam. Make sure the fold-over elastic piece extends outside the side seam.

2 **Baste the elastic.** Place the open elastic on the wrong side, aligning the centre fold-over ridge with the edge of the fabric. Attach the elastic from the right side using a basting stitch. An edge presser foot makes this easier. Stretch the elastic gently so that it shapes around the curves.

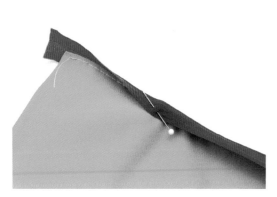

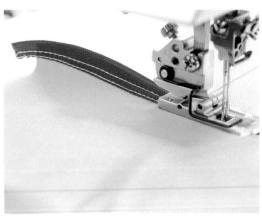

3 **Fold over and pin.** Place a few pins to keep the elastic in place.

4 **Coverstitch the elastic.** Start at the edge of the extended fold-over elastic. Sew close to the edge. You don't need to stretch out the elastic in this step, it should be done during the basting stage (step 2).

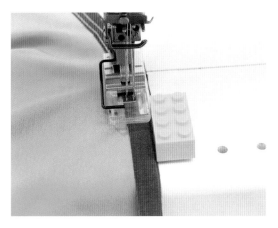

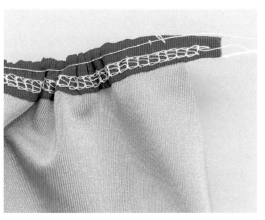

5 **Tools for sewing straight.** Place a seam guide or a piece of Lego attached with adhesive Blu-Tack outside the upper edge of the elastic. A clear presser foot also helps to stitch the fold-over elastic evenly.

6 **Remove the basting stitches.** Pull the thread from the back of the seam.

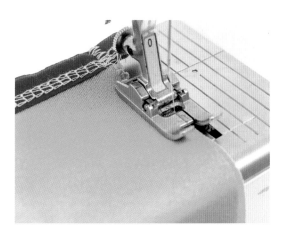

7 **Sew the side seam.** Just sew over the elastic edges when sewing the side seam. This method is commonly used on ready-to-wear underwear.

8 **The finished seam.** As an option, sew some tack stitches over the seam allowance from the right side to keep the seam in place.

ELASTIC OPENINGS

Use this professional method to finish openings on underwear and swimwear. The trick is to get the settings right, especially when stitching over thicker elastic, which can cause skipped stitches and uneven feeding. If you have problems with skipped stitches try using clear elastic instead of regular knit elastic.

SUPPLIES

- Size 90/14 needles
- Narrow knit elastic or clear elastic. Use chlorine-resistant swimsuit elastic for swimwear
- Serger thread for the needle threads
- Woolly nylon or serger thread in the looper
- Wide or narrow 2-needle coverstitch

DETERMINING THE ELASTIC LENGTH

NECKLINES: The elastic should be the same length as the garment neckline.

WAISTS: The elastic should be the same length as the garment or slightly shorter, but not less than 85% in most cases. Test and see what feels comfortable.

LEG OPENINGS: On swimwear and underwear, the elastic should be shorter in the back and about the same length as the garment in the front. For instance, use 80–85% length in the back and 95–100% in the front.

TIPS FOR COVERSTITCHING ELASTIC

- Use size 90/14 needles to prevent skipped stitches
- Increase the stitch length
- Increase the presser foot pressure
- Lower the differential feed
- Use a hump-jumper to lift the presser foot over bulky seams
- Place the overlapped elastic slightly outside the seam to reduce bulk

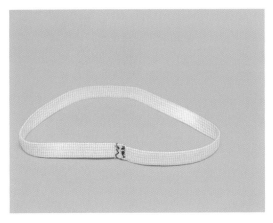

1 **Close the elastic.** Overlap the elastic and stitch it together with two rows of zigzag stitches. Backstitch to secure the seams.

2 **Divide and pin the elastic.** Pin the elastic on the wrong side, making sure the length of the elastic is properly distributed. On necklines and waists, divide the elastic into quarters. On leg openings, the elastic should be stretched out more in the back (see *Determining the elastic length* on page 106)

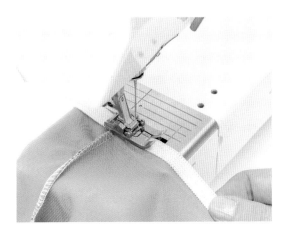

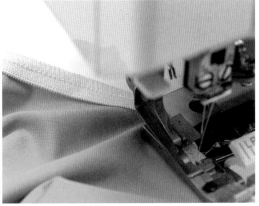

3 **Option 1: Use a zigzag stitch.** Using a medium zigzag stitch on the sewing machine, sew the elastic and stretch as you sew. Make sure the elastic edge aligns with the edge of the fabric.

4 **Option 2: Serge the elastic.** Use a 3-thread overlock and disengage the cutting knife so that it won't cut into the elastic. The edge of the elastic should align with the edge of the fabric. Stretch as necessary.

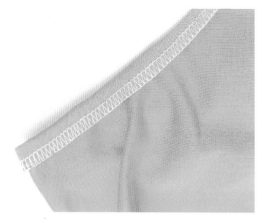

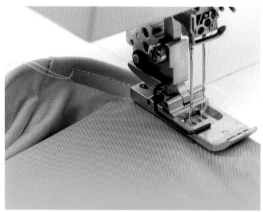

5 **Fold the elastic.** Use the inner edge of the elastic as a guide for the fold. The elastic should be fully covered by the fabric.

6 **Coverstitch the elastic.** Start just after a seam to avoid skipped stitches. On leg openings, stitch from the inner leg to the front. The stitch should be sewn close the inner edge of the fold. Stretch when needed.

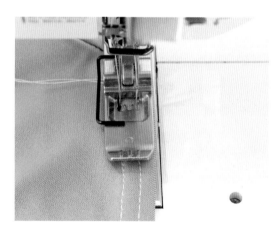

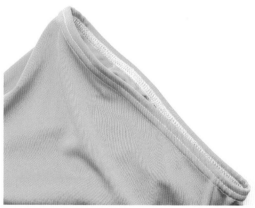

7 **Overlap the stitch.** Sew over the start of the seam for about 2.5 cm/ 1 in and then secure the stitch using your preferred method.

8 **The finished opening.** Here the front is sewn 1:1 and the back elastic is 85% of the back leg opening.

LINGERIE ELASTIC

Lingerie elastic is soft and usually has a picot edge. Use this elastic to finish waist, arm, leg openings and necklines. The method shown here is for folded and topstitched elastic. But the method for stretch lace (see page 100) can also be used.

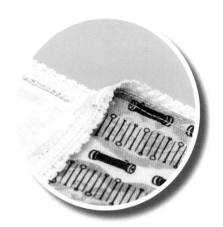

DETERMINING THE LENGTH

NECKLINES: The lingerie elastic should be the same length as the garment neckline.

WAISTS: The lingerie elastic should be the same length or just slightly shorter than the garment waist.

LEG OPENINGS: On underwear, the elastic could be slightly shorter in the back and around the same length as the garment in the front. For instance, use around 90% of the length in the back and 95–100% in the front.

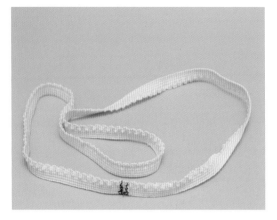

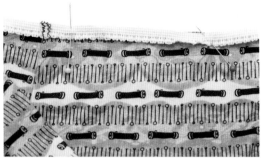

1 **Close the elastic.** Overlap the elastic and stitch it together with two rows of zigzag stitches. Backstitch to secure the seams.

2 **Pin the elastic.** With the picot edge placed downwards, pin the elastic on the right side, making sure the length of the elastic is properly distributed (see *Determining the elastic length* on page 106).

3 **Option 1: Use a zigzag stitch.** Using a medium zigzag stitch on the sewing machine; sew the elastic and stretch if necessary. The lower edge of the elastic should align with the edge of the fabric.

4 **Option 2: Serge the elastic.** Use a 3-thread overlock and disengage the cutting knife so that it won't cut into the elastic. The edge of the elastic should align with the edge of the fabric. Stretch as necessary.

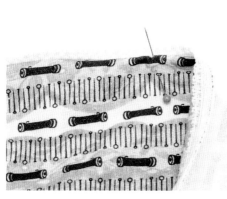

5 **Fold back and pin the elastic.** Fold so that the picot edge extends outside the fold.

6 **Coverstitch the elastic.** Start just after a seam to avoid skipped stitches. The stitch should be sewn close to the lower edge of the lingerie elastic. Stretch as you sew if needed.

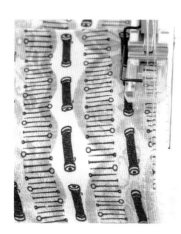

7 **Overlap the stitch.** Sew over the start of the coverstitch for about 2.5 cm (1 in) and then secure the stitch using your preferred method.

8 **The finished lingerie elastic opening.** This soft type of elastic is very comfortable to wear and is often a better choice for underwear than regular elastic.

"You can do so much more than just hem knit garments"

COVERSTITCH EXPERT

Gail Patrice Yellen

Gail Patrice Yellen teaches classes and workshops across the US, including several online classes, such as a coverstitch class on Craftsy.com. She is also the author of the book Serger Essentials. Experimenting with all types of embellishments is a favourite pastime and here Gail shares her best tips on how to master the coverstitch machine.

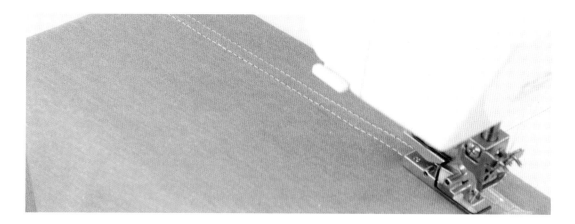

A lot of people buy a coverstitch machine to hem knits. But, as you show in your Craftsy class there, are other uses too. Share some your favourite unexpected ways we can use a coverstitch.

I teach serger/coverstitch classes all across the US and in 2015 was asked to do the Craftsy class. My focus was to demonstrate conventional, as well as creative, applications for the versatile coverstitch. It can do so much more than just hem knit garments

Using a thread palette to blend multiple threads in the chain looper, the looper side of the triple cover stitch is an easy and elegant way to embellish surfaces. Even a heavy (8–12 weight) decorative thread in the looper is lovely.

The wide coverstitch creates a perfect faux flat fell seam and is excellent for lapped seam construction. And I love using the belt loop binder, downturn feller, and binder attachments for necklines.

Some sewists express a frustration using the coverstitch machine. What are your top tips to make coverstitching less troublesome?

Whether overlocking or coverstitching, there are a few tips for success. My most important tip is to make a few samples to test stitch length, differential feed setting, needle selection, tension settings and which coverstitch works best, narrow, wide or triple, prior to working on a project.

Start with fresh needles and stitch at a slow to moderate speed. Stitching too fast can cause skipped stitches. Sewists tend to pull on the fabric in an effort to control it. This often results in stretched edges. Use a fabric guide for even hems and have all the needles sew both layers to minimise tunnelling.

A longer stitch length mimics ready-to-wear, 3.0, or longer depending on fabric weight. When hemming lightweight knit garments, cutting a strip of lightweight fusible knit interfacing, or woven fusible interfacing cut on the bias, gives the hem a bit more weight and stability and results in a nicer finished appearance.

GAIL'S TOP COVERSTITCH TIPS

Sewing bindings

Stitching binding takes some practice but the results are worth it. Follow the manufacturer's cutting instructions for the correct width of your strip. But be aware that different fabrics may require slightly different widths.

Test using a long strip of the fabric. Stitch length should be 3.5-4. It sounds long; however, you will be stitching through five layers–two double folds of binding and your neckline edge.

Don't allow the binding strip to stretch as it feeds through the attachment or hangs off the edge of your table. Check out my *Serger Tip Clip* on YouTube to see it in action!

Sewing over bulky layers

Stitching over bulky layers requires a longer stitch length and larger size needle, such as a 90/14. You may also need to adjust the presser foot pressure. Test on scrap fabric. Stitch slowly. When crossing seam intersections, slow down, increase stitch length and hand walk the needles over the seam allowance.

After you stitch past the seam allowance, pause and re-set stitch to your original length. Flip the seam allowance under the hem to offset from the body of the garment's seam allowance.

Avoiding skipped stitches

If your stitch formation isn't perfect, there could be several reasons. If you haven't changed your needles in 4 6 hours of stitching, replace with a fresh ones.

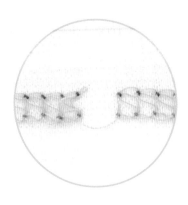

Some knit fabrics, especially those with Lycra, Spandex or Elastine, require a stretch needle. Resist pulling your fabric either from the front or back of the presser foot. When sewists pull from behind the presser foot, they often pull the fabric faster than the serger can fully form a stitch, thus skipping stitches.

FOLDED AND STITCHED NECKLINE

The easiest way to finish a neckline on a knit top using a coverstitch machine. Works well on both round and boat necklines. All you need to do is fold the fabric inwards and coverstitch.

>> **SUPPLIES**

- Wide or narrow 2-needle coverstitch
- Size 80/12 or 90/14 needles

1 **Fold and press the neckline inwards.** The seam allowance should only be around 1 cm (3/8 in). If it's wider, it will be difficult to get the fabric to lie flat.

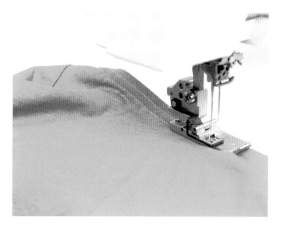

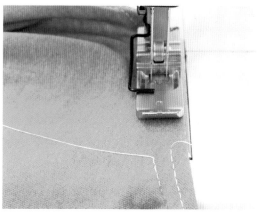

2 **Coverstitch the neckline.** Stitch so that the looper thread covers the edge of the fabric on the reverse side. Start sewing on the back just before the shoulder seam. You can use either a narrow or wide 2-needle coverstitch seam.

3 **Overlap the seam.** Stitch over the beginning seam for a few stitches to close the seam. Use the pull method described on pages 76–77 to then secure and finish the seam.

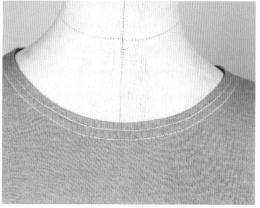

4 **The finished neckline.** Notice the overlapping stitches to the left; this is where the seam is secured. This method creates a clean, non-bulky finishing without having to use binding or ribbing and is commonly used on ready-to-wear jersey tops.

SINGLE LAYER BINDING

A simple binding technique that is less bulky than the classic double layer binding. It's also easier to learn, which makes it a great beginner method for binding. Serging the edge beforehand helps control the binding when topstitched and also creates a neat finish, but is not required.

1 **Prepare the binding.** The width of the strip should be around 3.5 times the width of the finished binding plus seam allowance. Also, make the binding a bit longer than the neckline, as it will make the binding easier to handle when sewing. Overcast one side of the binding using either the 3-thread serger overlock or a decorative sewing machine stretch stitch (optional).

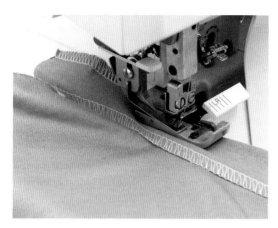

2 **Attach the binding.** You'll need to leave one shoulder or side seam open. Right sides facing, attach the binding using a serger or sewing machine. Stretch the binding gently as you sew, especially around the curves.

3 **Prepare for topstitching.** Fold the binding over the seam allowance. Press with an iron on low heat if the fabric can handle it.

TIP: Hand baste or use basting glue to keep the binding in place when topstitching.

4 **Coverstitch the binding.** Use a narrow or wide 2-needle coverstitch or a 1-needle chainstitch to topstitch the binding in place. Sew close to the edge. Close the binding by sewing together the open seam afterwards (see *Double layer knit binding* on pages 124–125).

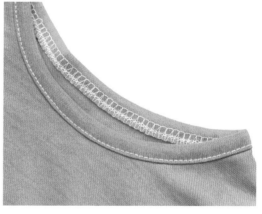

5 **The finished neckline.** With this method, you will achieve a neat and non-bulky finish. The chainstitch used in this example is a great choice for any type of narrow neckline finish.

BINDING WITH A TRIMMED EDGE

This single layer binding option is perfect for getting an even finish on the reverse side. With this method, you make the binding extra wide and then remove excess fabric after you have topstitched the binding. You'll be using a straighter stitch when attaching the binding but it will not pop, as you are securing the binding using a coverstitch seam.

>> **SUPPLIES**

- Knit fabric (both self-fabric and ribbing will work)
- Sewing machine
- Wide or narrow 2-needle coverstitch
- Size 80/12 or 90/14 needles
- Rotary cutter or a pair of sharp scissors

1 **Cut the binding.** Cut a rectangular strip crosswise that is both longer and wider than the finished neckline binding. To calculate the width, multiply the desired finished width of the binding by 3, then add around 3 cm (1 ¼ in) extra width or more; the excess fabric will be removed after sewing. The length of the strip should be the length of the area you are binding plus at least 5 cm (2 in) extra.

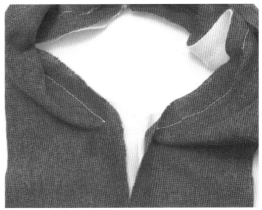

2 **Attach the binding.** Use a longer straight stitch or a narrow zigzag and sew the binding to the garment, wrong side up, right sides facing. Stitch as far from the edge as you want the width of the binding to be. Stretch as you sew so that the binding lies flat in the curves.

3 **Leave the ends open.** You need to leave 2.5 cm (1 in) of the binding open on each side in order to close the seam.

4 **Close the opening.** Stretch out the fabric slightly and sew the edges together to create a closed binding. Trim the extra fabric on the seam allowance.

5 **Attach the remaining binding.** Sew right sides facing over the seam allowance that is pressed apart. Stretch as you sew.

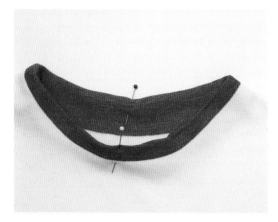

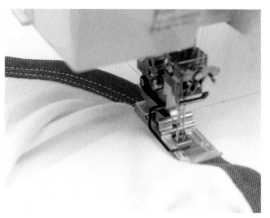

6 **Prepare for coverstitching.** Fold over the binding and pin it in place. You can also baste or use basting glue to keep the fabric in place when coverstitching.

7 **Coverstitch the binding.** You can use either a 2-needle narrow or wide coverstitch. A 3-needle coverstitch can also work.

8 **Cut away the excess fabric.** Cut carefully, just below the stitch, using either a rotary cutter or a sharp pair of scissors.

9 **The finished neckline.** This method is the least bulky of all binding finishes and, with practice you'll be able to cut very evenly and close to the seam.

DOUBLE LAYER KNIT BINDING

A double layer binding closely mimics the look of ready-to-wear binding, but without needing a binder attachment. Also called French binding, this finishing technique looks very neat on the inside as well. It can, however, be bulky so for best results, only use this method on thin, lightweight knit fabrics.

> **SUPPLIES**
>
> - Knit fabric (both self-fabric and ribbing will work)
> - Wide or narrow 2-needle coverstitch or a chainstitch
> - Size 80/12 or 90/14 needles
> - Sewing machine or serger
> - Rotary cutter or a pair of sharp scissors

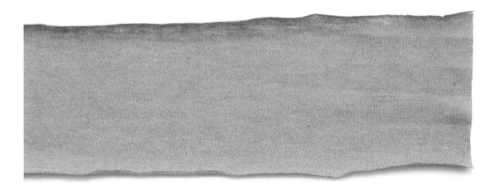

1 **Cut a rectangular strip of fabric crosswise.**
Width: 6 x the finished binding width + around 1 cm (3/8 in) extra. The extra width will compensate for when the fabric is folded in several layers and stretched out.

Length: The length of the neckline + 10 cm extra (4 in). The extra length makes the binding easier to sew. Note that the binding will be stretched out when sewing and one garment seam needs to be left open when using this method.

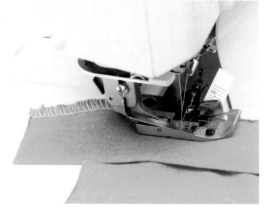

2 **Fold the binding.** If the fabric can handle it, ironing over the fold will make the fold more crisp.

3 **Attach the binding.** Use a serger seam or a sewing machine stretch seam. Let 5 cm (2 in) extend outside the edge. Sew the binding, right sides facing. The width of the seam should be the same width as the folded binding. Stretch as you sew so that the binding will lie flat in the curves.

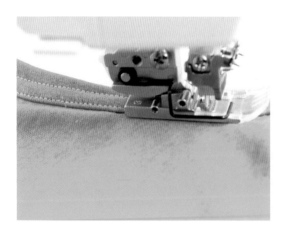

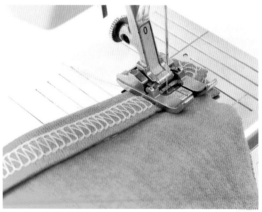

4 **Fold and topstitch tho binding.** Use a narrow or wide 2-needle coverstitch or a 1-needle chainstitch. Stitch close to the edge. A clear presser foot can be helpful.

5 **Close the binding.** To finish the binding, you need to close the seam that you left open. Start by sewing over the bulky binding area using a regular sewing machine and a straight stitch. This will make closing the seam easier.

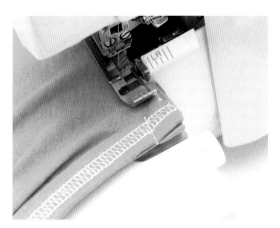

6 **Sew the remaining seam.** Sew from the opposite directions using a serger or sewing machine stretch seam. Either stop at the straight seam or sew the remaining seam, close to the outer edge. This solves the bulk problem.

7 **Stitch down the seam allowance.** To keep the seam allowance in place, sew a vertical tack seam over the seam allowance. Do this from the right side.

8 **The finished binding.** Using the French binding method is what will yield the most professional-looking results without having to use a binder attachment. Just remember to stretch the fabric when sewing and to only use lighter knit fabrics to avoid bulk.

BINDER ATTACHMENT KNIT BINDING

This is the professional way to do a knit binding finish on clothes. The attachments do either 3-fold or 4-fold and will fold and sew the binding in one go. Binder attachments will require some practice before you can fully master this tool.

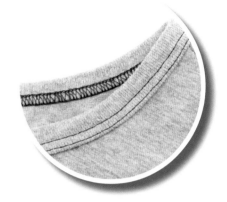

SUPPLIES

- Knit fabric (both self-fabric and ribbing will work)
- Tape binder attachment
- Narrow or wide 2-needle coverstitch or a chainstitch
- Size 80/12 or 90/14 needles
- Rotary cutter or a pair of sharp scissors

TIPS FOR USING A COVERSTITCH BINDER

- Use size 90/14 needles if you get skipped stitches, especially if the layers are thick
- Increase the stitch length, 3–4 is recommended
- Experiment with the presser foot pressure, try both lowering and increasing it to see what works best
- Roll the tape on an empty toilet roll and put it on a paper towel stand. This will help to feed the tape evenly and keep it from collapsing before it is fed into the binder attachment

- Use a piece of Lego or a magnetic seam guide to keep the binding from slipping
- Don't pull the binding when sewing. Just gently guide the binding back in place if it is slipping
- A clear presser foot makes it easier to sew straight as you can see how the binding lines up and when the tape starts to slip
- Lower the differential feed; this can make the feeding of the binding easier

1 **Cut the strip.** Use the width recommended for your binder (the more exact you can cut them, the better the result). Generally, you should cut the strips cross-wise, along the direction of the stretch.

2 **Shape the edge.** Cut the strip end as a triangle for easy insertion into the binder attachment.

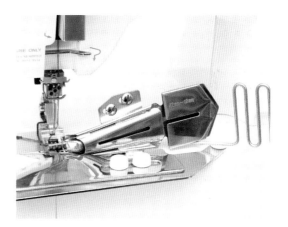

3 **Roll the strip.** To get the strip to feed evenly into the binder and keep it from collapsing, roll the strip on a toilet roll and place it on a paper towel stand or some other device.

4 **Attach the binder.** Follow the instructions of your particular model. If you have a generic binder, use Blu-Tack or tape to keep it in place.

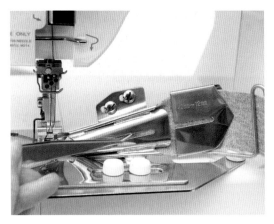

5 **Pull the fabric through the binder attachment.** With the wrong side of the fabric facing you, use a needle, awl, or tweezers to pull it through the narrow tube opening.

6 **Place the strip underneath the presser foot.** Pinch the edge and then pull the binding underneath the presser foot. For best results, have around 2.5–5 cm (1-2 in) of tape behind the presser foot.

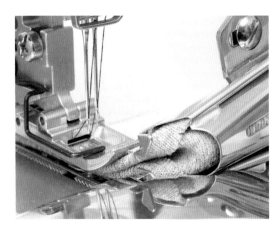

7 **Make sure that the strip is properly folded.** On some binder attachments, you can adjust the balance of the fold. The upper fold should generally be slightly wider than the lower fold, but test and see what works for you.

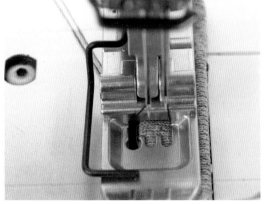

8 **Align the folded tape with the needles.** The edge of the tape should be slightly to the left of the middle needle.

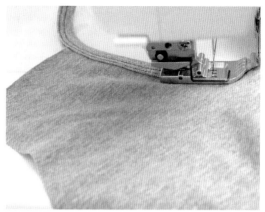

9 **Start sewing the tape.** Don't insert the garment fabric until you have made sure everything looks okay. Insert the edge of the garment fabric into the fold.

TIP: Use a piece of Lego to prevent the binding from slipping. Blu-Tack or tape will keep the Lego in place.

10 **Sew carefully.** Don't pull or yank the tape when sewing as it will mess everything up. Just gently guide the tape. If it is slipping, use an awl or tweezers to guide the binding straight again.

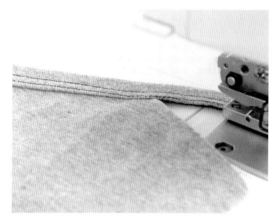

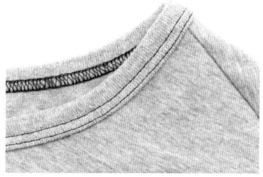

11 **Keep sewing over the edge.** When you are finished, continue sewing over the binding; you will cut off the extra afterwards. Finish the application by closing the seam you left open (see *Double layer knit binding* on pages 124–125).

12 **The finished binding.** This method can be tricky to master, but the result will be very professional. Try to get the reverse looper positioned so that it covers the edge on the inside.

BELT LOOPS

In the garment industry, belt loops are sewn on a cover-stitch machine. This is done using a folding attachment, but if you don't have an attachment, you can achieve a similar result using a piece of cardboard to create evenly folded loops.

>> **SUPPLIES**

- Regular sewing thread for the needles (some domestic coverstitch machines can't handle topstitch thread in the needles)
- Serger thread for the looper
- 2-needle wide coverstitch
- Size 90/14 needles
- A piece of cardboard

1 **Cut a piece of cardboard.** The width should be the same as the finished belt loops, around 1 cm (2/5 in) is a common width. The length of the piece should ideally be as long as all the belt loops plus seam allowances. Draw a line in the middle with a pencil.

2 **Cut the belt loop strip.** The fabric should be cut lengthwise. Cut a strip that is twice the finished width plus a few millimetres extra to compensate for the fold.

3 **Fold the loop.** Align the fabric edges with the line on the cardboard. Press with an iron to shape the fabric around the cardboard strip. Remove the cardboard strip after pressing.

4 **Stitch the belt loops.** The needles should hit the fabric on the first stitch.

5 **Make sure you sew in the middle.** Use the edges of the presser foot as a guide. You can also use a separate seam guide or a piece of Lego attached with Blu-Tack or tape.

6 **The finished loop.** Cut the loops into pieces of equal length and attach them to your garment.

BELT LOOPS USING A FOLDER

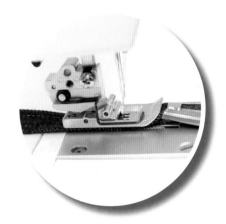

Using a belt loop folding attachment, you can make professional-looking belt loops in just a few minutes. Some coverstitch machine brands have this tool in their accessory range, but you can also use a generic folder and attach it with tape.

⟫ SUPPLIES

- A belt loop folder
- Regular sewing thread for the needles (some domestic coverstitch machines can't handle topstitch thread in the needles)
- Serger thread for the looper
- 2-needle wide coverstitch
- Size 90/14 needles

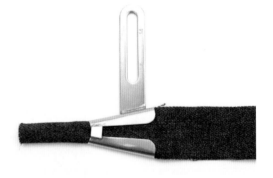

1 **Cut the belt loop strip.** The fabric should be cut along the grainline. Cut a strip that is twice the finished width, plus a tiny little extra, if the folder has edges that meet in the middle. If the loop attachment has edges overlap, add the extra width according to the instructions.

2 **Insert the strip into the folder.** Pull out around 5 cm (2 in) so that the presser foot can fully grab the fabric when you are coverstitching.

3 **Stitch the belt loop.** Attach the folder and insert the folded loop underneath the presser foot. The needles should hit the fabric on the first stitch.

4 **Make sure you stitch in the middle.** Move the folder slightly if needed.

5 **The finished loop piece.** Cut the loop into pieces of equal length and attach them to your garment.

CHAINSTITCHED JEANS HEM

According to many denim connoisseurs, proper jeans should be hemmed with a chainstitch and not a straight stitch, both because it is considered an old-school method, and because a chainstitch ages into a subtle wave that is called a roping effect.

The only drawback is that a chainstitch is more prone to unravelling, so make sure you secure the seam properly.

SUPPLIES

- Regular sewing thread for the needles (some domestic coverstitch machines can't handle topstitch thread in the needles)
- Serger or regular thread for the looper
- 1-needle chainstitch set-up
- Size 90/14 needles

Preparation

Sew together the side seams. You can leave the hem unfinished or overcast it with an overlock or zigzag stitch. A raw unfinished edge will be less bulky and it won't fray once the seam is folded and stitched.

Also, do a sample on your chosen fabric before hemming to get the settings right. You will most likely have to change the tension, decrease the differential feed, and increase the presser foot pressure when sewing over heavier woven fabrics such as denim.

1 **Fold and press the hem.** The standard jeans hem width is around 1.5 cm (5/8 in).

2 **Fold and press again.** Let the edge of the fabric be your guide when folding the second time, you don't need to measure the fold this time.

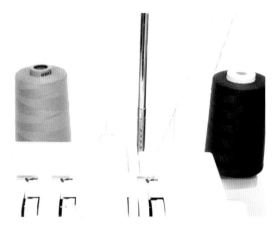

3 **Prepare the machine.** Use sewing thread in the needle and serger or regular sewing thread in the looper. The thread to the left in the picture is regular sewing machine thread that comes on cones. Use size 90/14 needles and set your machine for single needle chainstitch.

4 **Start sewing just after the in-seam.** Because a coverstitch machine is sensitive to bulk, don't start by sewing over a seam.

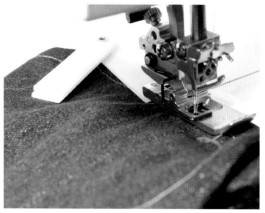

5 **Stitch close to the upper folded edge.** Make sure you feed the fabric evenly; don't tug it.

6 **Use a hump-jumper when sewing over the side seams.** Place the tool underneath the presser foot to level the foot; this will ensure that the fabric is fed evenly and prevent skipped stitches.

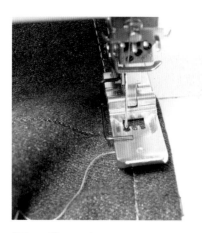

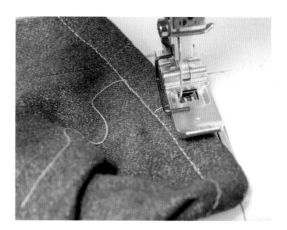

7 **Close the seam.** Let the chainstitch overlap for a few stitches.

8 **Remove the garment.** Release the threads, pinch the seam ends between your fingers and carefully remove the garment.

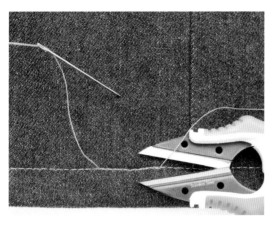

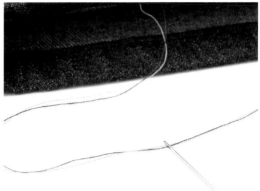

9 **Prepare for securing the threads.**
Pull the needle thread to the reverse
side using a sewing needle. Cut away
the beginning thread; this does not
need to be secured

10 **Insert the looper thread.** Once the
needle is on the reverse side; insert
the end looper thread so that both
the end needle thread and looper
thread is in the needle eye.

11 **Secure the end threads.** Tie the
threads into a knot using the needle
and secure the knot by attaching it to
the fabric. Cut the surplus thread.

12 **The finished hem.** As you can see
there is already a subtle wave on
the inside of the hem. This is the
trademark of jeans hemmed with a
chainstitch and it will become more
pronounced over time.

RIBBING CUFFS AND NECKBAND

The trick when sewing neckbands and cuffs is to use notches so that the ribbing is evenly distributed across the opening. After attaching the ribbing, the seam allowance is stitched down using a coverstitch, which creates a very professional finish and keeps the seam in place.

>> **SUPPLIES**

- Narrow or wide 2-needle coverstitch or a 1-needle chainstitch
- Ribbing, interlock, or self-fabric
- Sewing machine or a serger
- Size 80/12 or 90/14 needles
- Rotary cutter or a pair of sharp scissors

DETERMINING THE SIZE OF THE RIBBING

- In general, ribbing should always be shorter than the garment width. Here are some general guidelines, but it's a good idea to sew a sample to make sure it works
- **Neckline**: 65-75% (depends on the recovery of the ribbing and how curved the neckline is)
- **Sleeveless arm openings:** Around 80%
- **Waist rib:** 95 % for a smooth finish that fits in with current fashion. Around 80% for a more retro look.
- **Cuffs:** 95% for a smooth modern finish,; 80% if you want gathers like the clasic, retro style, of college sweaters and sweatpants

MAKING NOTCHES FOR EVEN RIBBING

- Add notches on the ribbing that correspond with the garment. For instance, on a neckline, add notches mid-back, mid-front, and at the shoulder seams
- If your rib is 75% of the neckline length, the notches on the ribbing should also be 75% of the corresponding distance on the garment neckline. For instance if your mid-back to shoulder distance is 10 cm on your garment, the corresponding ribbing length should be 7.5 cm

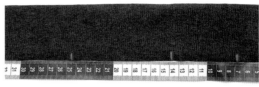

1 **Cut the ribbing.** Ideally, use a ruler and a rotary cutter to cut the ribbing because it creates the most even ribbing piece. But a paper pattern piece and a pair of scissors will work too, just make sure the scissors are sharp and that you cut straight.

2 **Mark notches on the ribbing.** Mark notches that correspond to mid-back, shoulder seams, and mid-front. If your rib is 75% of the neckline length, the notches on the ribbing should also be 75% of the corresponding distance on the garment.

3 **Sew and fold the ribbing band.** Use either a serger stitch or a sewing machine stretch seam. Fold the ribbing.

TIP: To create a flat fold, clip the seam allowance at the fold and press in opposite directions if the seam is durable enough.

4 **Match up the notches.** Add corresponding notches on your garment and align them with the notches on your ribbing.

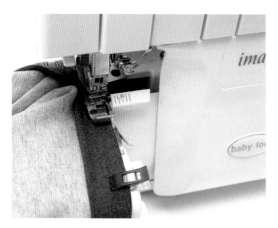

5 **Attach the ribbing.** Use either a serger or a sewing machine stretch seam to attach the ribbing. Stretch the ribbing while sewing, making sure the notches align.

6 **Press the ribbing flat.** After sewing, it's a good idea to press the ribbing on a low setting to make sure the ribbing lies flat and to remove any creases. Test the fabric first to see that it can tolerate an iron.

7 **Coverstitch over the ribbing.** Stitch either over the seam allowance only or use the straddle position (see pages 84–87 for tutorials on both techniques). Use a narrow or wide 2-needle coverstitch or a 1-needle chainstitch to stitch down the ribbing.

8 **The finished neckband.** Using a coverstitch seam to stitch the ribbing seam allowance down is a standard practice in the garment industry.

TIP: Use contrasting thread in the needles for a decorative effect.

SWEATSHIRT V-APPLIQUÉ

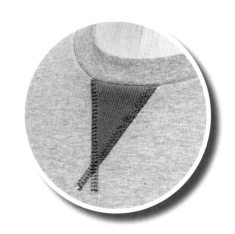

This triangle insert has been a traditional feature on sweatshirts since they first became popular during the first half of the 1900s. In the garment industry these are often done with a top-cover-stitch machine and a proper gusset insert. But you can also use a regular coverstitch machine to achieve a similar effect using reverse coverstitching and a triangle appliqué.

Preparation

Cut a triangle. A common size for the insert is around 4–6 cm (1 3/5–2 2/5 in) wide at the base and around 6 cm (2 2/5 in) long from the base to the tip. Shape the base so that it follows the roundness of the neckline.

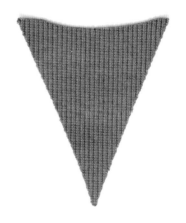

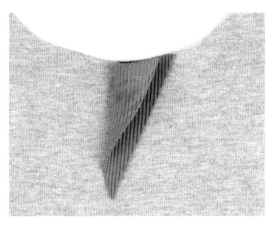

1 **Place the triangle insert.** Use basting glue or regular water-soluble stick glue to keep the triangle in place. Make sure it is placed in the middle and is straight.

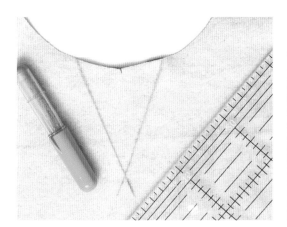

2 **Mark an V on the reverse side.** A common length is around 10 cm (4 in). Draw the lines just outside the insert. Let the lines intersect below the midpoint to create an X.

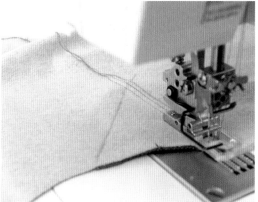

3 **Stitch the insert.** Start at the lower point of the first line. A 3-needle stitch will create a more decorative stitch, but a wide 2-needle stitch will also work. The outer needle should follow the line marking.

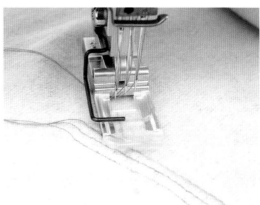

4 **Stop sewing at the edge of the neckline.** Use your preferred method to secure the threads. This is how the 3-thread coverstitch looks on the right side.

5 **Repeat on the other line.** Make sure both rows are perpendicular to each other.

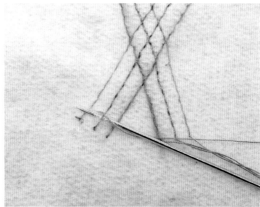

6 **Pull the looper thread to the reverse side.** Use a sewing needle.

7 **Attach the thread to a stitch on the reverse side.**

8 **Cut the needle threads.** The beginning of a coverstitch seam is automatically locked and won't unravel.

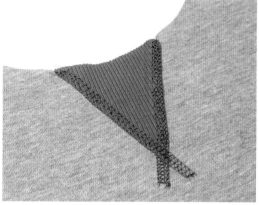

9 **The insert from the right side.** Now sew the sweater as you normally would.

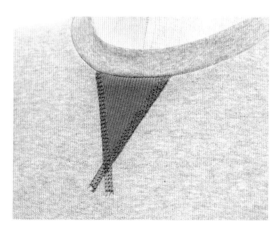

10 **The finished sweater.** The neckline ribbing will enclose the edges and the lower threads will not unravel.

11 **TIP.** You can also stitch a decorative V without using an insert. Just draw the lines as described in step 2 and stitch using the same method.

DECORATIVE SIDE POCKET

This distinct pocket construction utilises two coverstitch techniques; binding and reverse cover-stitching. It's a great addition to loungewear and activewear, and has many more uses too!

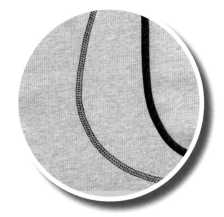

SUPPLIES

- Ribbing
- Garment fabric
- A 3-needle or wide 2-needle coverstitch
- Serger thread for the needles
- Serger thread or woolly nylon in the looper
- Thread for basting or basting glue (optional)

DRAFT THE POCKETS

1. Place tissue paper on the garment pattern and trace the side, waist and grainline

2. Draw the shape of the pocket on the paper (blue line)

3. Draw the pocket opening (orange line)

4. Trace the pocket following the blue line

5. Cut out the pocket opening on the original pattern piece using the orange line (A)

6. Trace a separate piece for the pocket piece (B)

7. Add notches and seam allowances (if they are not included in the pattern)

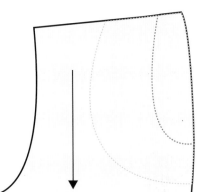

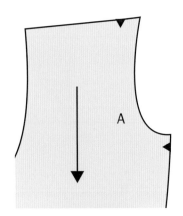

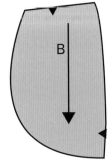

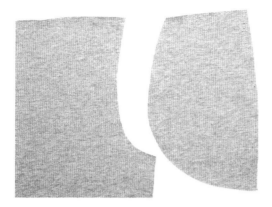

1 **Cut the front and pocket piece.**

2 **Cut the binding.** A recommended width is around 2.5 cm (1 in), including seam allowance. The piece needs to be around 10 cm (4 in) longer than the pocket opening.

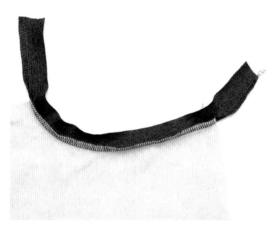

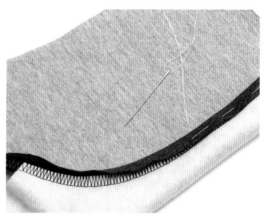

3 **Attach the binding.** Use an overlock stitch and stretch the binding in the curves so that it will lie flat when turned and stitched. Have at least 5 cm (2 in) surplus binding on each side. This will make topstitching easier.

4 **Fold the binding.** Baste the binding with large stitches or use washable basting glue to keep the fold in place.

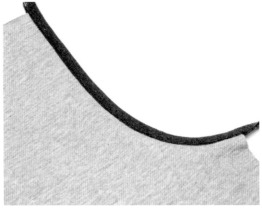

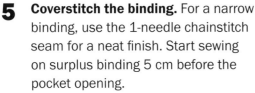

5 **Coverstitch the binding.** For a narrow binding, use the 1-needle chainstitch seam for a neat finish. Start sewing on surplus binding 5 cm before the pocket opening.

6 **The stitched binding.** Now it's time to add the pocket piece.

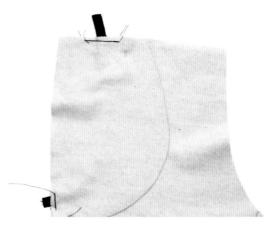

7 **Attach the pocket piece.** Make sure it aligns with the notches. Baste the edges to keep the pocket in place during ɔcwing.

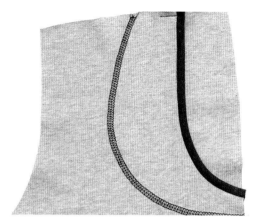

8 **Reverse coverstitch the pocket.** Stitch around the pocket using a 3-needle coverstitch or a 2-needle wide stitch. The outer needle should sew along the edge of the pocket.

9 **The finished pocket.** Next steps are sewing together the side seams and attaching the waistband.

COVERSTITCH RESOURCES

COVERSTITCH RESOURCE COLLECTION

thelaststitch.com/coverstitching

The go-to place for all things coverstitching and the companion resource for this book. Here you'll find reviews of coverstitch machines and tools, video guides, step-by-step tutorials and much more

OTHER RESOURCES

Coverstitching by Hilde
coverstitching.com

Coverstitch Facebook Sewing Discussion Group
facebook.com/groups/Hilde.Coverstitch

A guide to coverstitching by Melissa Fehr
seamwork.com/issues/2015/06

Stitches and Seams coverstitch guides
stitchesandseams.blogspot.com

Craftsy Coverstitch class by Gail Yellen
craftsy.com/class/coverstitch-basics-beyond

OTHER BOOKS BY THE AUTHOR

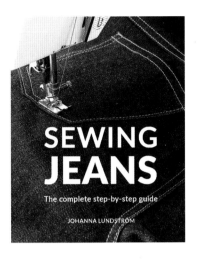

Sewing Jeans:
The complete step-by-step guide

This comprehensive book takes you through the entire process from picking the right fabric and notions to completing a pair of jeans that will rival high-end denim brands.

Take your skills to the next level with the help of clearly illustrated, step-by-step instructions and easy to follow techniques.

Johanna Lundström (2020)

Sewing Activewear: How to make your own professional-looking athletic wear

The ultimate sewing guide for creating your own workout clothes that are both functional and stylish.

Fully illustrated step-by-step tutorials covering everything from beginner techniques to professional fashion industry methods.

Johanna Lundström (2017)

Perfekt Nähen mit der Coverlock:
Tipps, Tricks & Tutorials

The German version of Master the Coverstitch Machine.

Johanna Lundström
Stiebner Verlag (2020)

INDEX

NOTES